Speaking truth to power
Research and policy on lifelong learning

Edited by Frank Coffield

First published in Great Britain in 1999 by

The Policy Press
University of Bristol
34 Tyndall's Park Road
BRISTOL BS8 1PY
UK

Tel   +44 (0)117 954 6800
Fax   +44 (0)117 973 7308
E-mail tpp@bristol.ac.uk
http://www.bristol.ac.uk/Publications/TPP/

In association with the ESRC *Learning Society Programme*

ISBN 1 86134 147 4

Frank Coffield is Professor of Education in the Department of Education at the University of Newcastle. He is also currently the Director of the ESRC's programme *The Learning Society* (1994-2000).

Cover design by Qube Design Associates, Bristol.
Printed in Great Britain by Hobbs the Printers Ltd, Southampton.

Contents

Notes on contributors

Ms Jane Alderton is Senior Lecturer at the Institute of Nursing and Midwifery, University of Brighton. She has published research on knowledge use by nurses and midwives and interprofessional healthcare teams.

Professor David Ashton is Professor of Sociology at the Centre for Labour Market Studies, University of Leicester. His research interests are in the general field of education, training and employment. This includes the study of national systems of education, training and skill formation and the ways in which they are adapting to the pressures of globalisation. His other main interest is in the process of workplace learning, skill formation and performance improvement.

Professor Stephen Ball is Professor of Sociology of Education and Director of the Centre for Public Policy Research at King's College London. He is editor of the *Journal of Education Policy* and the author of several books on education policy including *Politics and policy making in education* (Routledge, 1990), *Education reform* (Open University Press, 1994) and, with Sharon Gewirtz and Richard Bowe, *Markets, choice and equity in education* (Open University Press, 1995).

Dr Will Bartlett is Reader in Social Economics at the School for Policy Studies, University of Bristol. He has carried out research on social policy, covering health and education reforms, and on comparative economic systems. He has published widely on various aspects of marketisation in western European welfare states and in the transition economies of Eastern Europe. He is co-

editor of *A revolution in social policy: Quasi-markets in the 1990s* (The Policy Press, 1998).

Dr Brendan Burchell is a Lecturer in the Faculty of Social and Political Sciences and a Fellow of Magdalene College at the University of Cambridge. His research interests include psychological and interdisciplinary approaches to labour market disadvantage.

Professor Frank Coffield has been Professor of Education in the Department of Education at the University of Newcastle since 1996, having previously worked at Durham and Keele Universities. He is currently Director of the ESRC's research programme into *The Learning Society* from 1994-2000. In 1997 he edited a report *A national strategy for lifelong learning* (Department of Education, University of Newcastle) and produced in 1999 *Breaking the consensus: Lifelong learning as social control* (Department of Education, University of Newcastle).

Mr Gerald Cole is a Research Fellow at the University of Sussex. He is the author of bestselling books on management, and has researched into the teaching of business studies and the assessment of professional competence.

Dr Therese Dowswell is a health service researcher with a special interest in the maternity services and the education and training of health services staff. Until recently Therese was a senior research fellow in the Department of Psychology at the University of Leeds. Inspired by participants in recent research projects, Therese is now a student nurse at the School of Health Studies at Bradford University.

Professor Michael Eraut is Professor of Education at the University of Sussex Institute of Education and directed one of the projects entitled 'Development of knowledge and skills in employment', as part of the ESRC's *Learning Society Programme*. He has published widely in the areas of professional and vocational education and about different kinds of knowledge.

Dr Alan Felstead is Director of Research and Senior Research Fellow at the Centre for Labour Market Studies, University of Leicester. He has published widely in the field of Employment Studies on issues such as the growth of 'non-standard' forms of employment, the process of skill formation and training policy. He has also carried out policy-related work for a range of clients including the Department for Education and Employment, the European Centre for the Development of Vocational Training and the European Union. He is currently a member of the Research Group of the government's Skills Task Force.

Professor Francis Green is Professor of Economics at the University of Kent at Canterbury. He has published a number of books and many papers on the role of education and training in the economy, on the impact of unions, on other areas of labour economics and on political economy. He has also written many reports for the British government's Department for Education and Employment, and is currently on the Research Group to the government's Skills Task Force.

Dr Jenny Hewison is a Senior Lecturer in the School of Psychology at the University of Leeds. Her teaching and research interests lie in health psychology, and in learning and behaviour change, with particular reference to staff and patients in the NHS.

Professor Maurice Kogan is Professor of Government and Social Administration (Emeritus) and Director of the Centre for the Evaluation of Public Policy and Practice, Brunel University. He is the author of several books and articles on education, higher education and science policy.

Dr Sheila Macrae is Research Fellow in the School of Education, King's College London working on a longitudinal study of young people in transition from school to work. She has been involved in a number of other research projects at King's, the Open University and elsewhere, and has a special interest in students with learning and behaviour difficulties.

Dr Meg Maguire is Senior Lecturer in the School of Education, King's College London. She is co-editor of *Becoming a teacher* (Open University Press, 1997) and author of a number of papers on the teaching profession and women teachers. She is deputy editor of the *Journal of Education Policy*, and is currently completing a book on primary schooling in the inner city.

Mrs Bobbie Millar is Academic Secretary in the School of Health Care Studies at the University of Leeds. At the beginning of the research she was Director of Academic Affairs at the Leeds College of Health and became involved in the project because the College provided education and training for a range of healthcare professionals. The project has been particularly useful for the School as it continues to develop its portfolio of programmes for lifelong learning to support NHS and other health providers.

Professor Teresa Rees is Professor of Labour Market Studies at the School for Policy Studies, University of Bristol. She has carried out research on the position of women in the labour market and on training programmes in both the UK and Europe. She has acted as advisor to the European Commission on mainstreaming equal opportunities and is Equal Opportunities Commissioner for Wales.

Mr Peter Senker has been a Senior Researcher in the Science Policy Research Unit and, more recently, the Institute of Education at the University of Sussex. He has published widely in the training of engineers and is now a visiting professor at the University of East London.

Introduction: past failures, present differences and possible futures for research, policy and practice

Frank Coffield

Introduction

There are many countries throughout the world where a report such as this could not be published. For here are teams of researchers who have been funded by the public purse, recording in detail serious inefficiencies, unjustifiable inequalities and unintended consequences in government policy. Certainly, the chapters which follow contain many constructive suggestions, new interpretations, new knowledge and alternative ways of thinking; but it would be foolish to deny that, taken together, they also constitute a powerful critique of current policy on lifelong learning. A curt and dismissive response from officialdom would be understandable. However, the claim that this government is creating a renaissance, a *Learning Age*, a genuine Learning Society in the UK, will in part be tested by the extent to which such friendly critics are not only tolerated and funded, but imaginatively and seriously involved in the development of better policy.

The latter suggestion should not be interpreted as belief in a simple linear model where research influences policy directly. An understanding of the relationship between research and policy is only marginally improved by referring to complex and dynamic interactions between the two. Rather, the challenge is to come to terms with "the messy realities of influence, pressure, dogma, expediency,

conflict, compromise, intransigence, resistance, error, opposition and pragmatism in the policy process" (Ball, 1990, p 9), within which research is only one of a host of competing interests.

These muddy waters have not, in my opinion, been purified or even clarified by two recent reports on educational research, the first commissioned by OFSTED (Tooley and Darby, 1998) and the second by the Department for Education and Employment (Hillage et al, 1998). Harold Silver has taken to task the main author of the second report, Jim Hillage, for claiming that the research and policy-making communities had drifted far apart in recent years: "It is misleading to suggest that the two communities had 'drifted apart'. They had never seriously been together" (Silver, 1999: forthcoming).

That conclusion is supported by Maurice Kogan in his magisterial overview of the impact of research on policy in the first chapter of this report. Looking back over the last 30 years, he argues that educational policies in the UK have not conformed:

... to a knowledge-based model, but to the heroic model which relies on value setters, such as Joseph, Clarke, Baker and Blunkett, who know what they want and set out to get it without recourse to supporting or opposing evidence. As Eric Forth put it "we don't need research to tell us what to do, we know that already".

Certainly the present government's advocacy of performance-related pay follows this tradition, as the case for reform is not being made on the basis of evidence but relies on the Secretary of State who "believe(s) passionately that it is the right change" (DfEE, 1998b, p 5).

One significant issue to which the Hillage report rightly drew attention was that current financial investment in educational research is insufficient to meet the demands now being made of it. Hillage et al give the percentage of 0.18 as the proportion of total public expenditure on education in 1991/92 which was devoted to education research and development. That percentage has barely improved from the figure of 0.12 for 1968-69, quoted by Nisbet and Broadfoot (1980, p 32). Such low provision repeated generation after generation has seriously affected research capacity because there has never been sufficient continuity in funding to create either a career structure for new/young researchers or a research ambience in Departments of Education, where those straight from teaching in schools could have been routinely trained in a range of research methods.

Moreover, the two reports have been used by influential figures to create the impression of a crisis in educational research which would justify determined intervention. The Chief Inspector of Schools, for instance, concluded that the Tooley and Darby report (which he commissioned without any peer-reviewed competition) had established that "much that is published is, on this analysis, at best no more than an irrelevance and distraction" (Woodhead, 1998, p 1). Similarly, the minister with responsibility for educational research wrote, in an article with the unnecessarily theological title of 'Resurrecting research to raise standards', that both reports had "concluded that research relating to schools is largely irrelevant and inaccessible, rarely informing policy and practice" (Clarke, 1998, p 8). The verdict of the research community, however, has been that the evidence produced by both reports is so weak (to put it mildly) that their conclusions are invalidated and generalisations based on them provide no basis for policy (see, for example, Hammersley, 1998; Goldstein, 1998; Edwards, 1998). What these two reports *have* created is a climate where research which is not immediately accessible, relevant and practical is likely to be discounted by politicians and their advisers with narrow definitions of these terms. As examples of research, the reports also exemplify the very weaknesses they identify in others.

The Learning Society Programme

In this turbulent and contentious atmosphere, five projects from *The Learning Society Programme* present the implications of their findings for policy. The chapters cover a wide range of topics from educational markets for 16- to 19-year-olds (Stephen Ball and colleagues in Chapter 3), to guidance services for adults (Will Bartlett and Teresa Rees in Chapter 6). The methods employed also vary from an intensive, qualitative study of how knowledge and skills develop in employment (Michael Eraut and colleagues in Chapter 2), to a major new survey of skill change in Britain over the last decade (Alan Felstead and colleagues in Chapter 5). The focus and locality of the studies also vary, from staff development in the National Health Service in Leeds (Jenny Hewison and colleagues in Chapter 4); to informal learning in engineering firms and insurance companies in the South East (Chapter 2); and to 'cut-throat' competition between secondary schools, Further Education Colleges and Training and Enterprise Councils in South West London (Chapter 3).

The present volume is the third in a series of four reports to be published by The Policy Press in 1998/99 on such themes as skill formation (the topic of the first report[1]), studies of Lifelong Learning in Europe (the topic of the second[2]) and informal learning (the fourth and final report[3]). *The Learning Society Programme* has also produced a contribution to the public debate on lifelong learning, entitled *A national strategy for lifelong learning* (Coffield, 1997); a collection of articles, which explored the concept of a learning society, in a special edition of the *Journal of Education Policy* (vol 12, no 5, November-December 1997); and a critique of government policy on lifelong learning, called *Breaking the consensus: Lifelong learning as social control* (Coffield, 1999). This report presents some further empirical findings and theoretical insights from five of the 14 projects which make up the Programme.

It may be appropriate to begin by briefly introducing *The Learning Society Programme* itself. The full title of the programme is *The Learning Society: knowledge and skills for employment* and the original specification described it as follows:

The Programme is a response to the growing national consensus that the UK needs to transform radically its thinking and practice in relation to education and training if it is to survive as a major economic power with a high quality of life, political freedom and social justice for all its citizens.

The aim of the Programme is to examine the nature of what has been called a learning society and to explore the ways in which it can contribute to the development of knowledge and skills for employment and other areas of adult life. The Programme focuses on post-compulsory education, training and continuing education in a wide variety of contexts, both formal and informal.

The Programme consists of 14 projects, involving over 50 researchers in teams spread throughout the UK from Belfast to Brighton. Each project has a different starting and finishing time and the Programme itself will run until March 2000. The five projects which present papers in this collection constitute a sub-group which were among the first to complete. It is also important to note that the researchers are here concentrating only on those particular aspects of their studies relevant to policy. Each project within the Programme will produce a comprehensive overview of their research in two edited collections of articles to be published by The Policy Press in 2000.

To employ a geological or mining metaphor, these five projects have sunk shafts into five different aspects of education, training and employment in Britain in order to test policy and practice on lifelong learning. They have brought back samples, specimens and cross-sections for examination and public discussion. In this introduction these have been grouped into four themes which appear and reappear in the chapters: implications for lifelong learning and the learning society; human capital theory; the individual as the target of policy; and practical recommendations. The introduction ends with a short discussion on possible future relations between research, policy and practice.

In sum, the articles in this report deal with a wide range of issues in a variety of contexts and in a number of different styles. But the broad themes being addressed by the researchers are the same in each case, whether the particular context is improving the quality of learning in engineering firms or providing vocational guidance for adults. What holds the chapters together are the shared objectives of exploring how the terms 'the learning society' and 'lifelong learning' have been operationalised in a particular area or sector, how effective current policy and practice are, and how these could be improved.

Implications for The Learning Society

Two of the main requirements made of all the projects funded by *The Learning Society Programme* were to treat the concept of the learning society as an issue for critical exploration and to maintain a policy focus. So it is no surprise that these obligations appear as recurrent themes in the chapters which follow. There is no attempt here to offer a comprehensive summary of all the policy implications suggested by the five projects, but rather to whet the reader's appetite by giving a few examples.

The first conclusion that Stephen Ball and his colleagues come to as a result of studying a particular education and training market post-16 is that policy for lifelong learning needs to begin at the age of three and not 16: "To a large extent the problems of poor participation, fragile motivation and status differentiation in post-16 education and training are rooted in compulsory education [which] … is not geared to inclusivity or achieving maximum post-16 participation". Lifelong learning is not, therefore, the preserve of adult educators, and policy must not concentrate on the post-compulsory sector, as both the Fryer Report (1997) and the government's Green Paper *The Learning Age* (DfEE, 1998a) tend to do.

The research team also concludes that "it is very difficult to see this market either as an effective means of raising standards or increasing participation or creating a national culture of learning". In more detail, within the education and training market in South West London which was studied, the behaviour of institutions:

> *... appears to generate a number of significant inefficiencies and duplications, it produces dis-coordination, it encourages segmentation, differentiation and exclusion, it inhibits information flow, it encourages short-termism, and it throws up ethical dilemmas, the resolution of which sometimes work against student interests.*

This research is not just recording some dysfunctional changes in managerial practices in post-compulsory education, but is providing hard evidence of the spread throughout the public sector of a new moral economy, based on a culture of self-interest (see Ball, 1997).

Only two conclusions have been quoted from a long and powerful chapter which contains many such implications for policy, and yet sufficient has been cited to indicate the scale of the task facing policy makers. An appropriate response will have to move beyond tinkering with minor defects to radical reform of fundamental flaws in the system.

Let us take one further example from the research of Will Bartlett and Teresa Rees into the provision of adult guidance services in England. Their argument – that adult careers guidance has become increasingly important as mobility between flexible jobs intensifies – is likely to be widely accepted. But are our current services geared up for such a flexible society?

> *On a national level the provision of adult guidance is patchy. The quality and range of services offered to users depend very much on the accident of where one happens to live.... The general fragmentation and patchiness of provision for adults are intensified in the provision of services for disadvantaged groups.*

Again, research is revealing serious inadequacies which will not be readily or cheaply rectified; at least the problems of inadequate information and advice have been recognised by the Labour government. And empirical data, produced by a major new survey of British workers funded by *The Learning Society Programme*, suggest that jobs in general are becoming more skilled and complex, for which more sophisticated careers guidance will be

necessary. This moves the discussion on neatly to the second theme and some more encouraging news.

Human capital theory

Alan Felstead and his colleagues in Chapter 5 provide robust information from their national survey which suggests a strong upward movement in the skills of the British workforce, especially among women, although the gender gap remains significant.

One of their major conclusions, that the mismatch between the demand and supply of *all* qualifications is "alarmingly high", has relevance for policy. In their own words, "in 1997 around one in five of those holding *any* qualifications reported that *no* qualification at all was required for the job they currently had" (original emphasis). Moreover, in the same year, three out of 10 graduates were in jobs for which a degree was not an entry requirement. It is vital that the central problem facing the UK in relation to skills is clearly enunciated: it is *not* the under-supply of qualified manpower but rather the low level of demand for it.

Economists continue to use the offensive term 'over-education' to describe this under-employment of individuals by employers or, more accurately, the over-recruitment by employers of individuals whose qualifications are higher than those required to get and do the job. The term is objectionable not only because it is difficult to imagine anyone who would be disadvantaged by too much education, but also because it locates the problem within individuals rather than with employers who are taking on able employees cheaply. This strategy also displaces those non-graduates who previously would have secured such jobs.

These findings are a clear reflection of the prevalence of low skilled jobs in the British labour market and of the persistently low demand from employers for graduates. Such over-qualified individuals represent, in economic terms, human capital in which considerable investment has been made (largely by the State), but which remains under-utilised. These new data support the evidence given to the Dearing Committee on

Higher Education by the Department for Education and Employment's own economists to the effect that the supply of new graduates would continue to exceed demand (Steel and Sausman, 1997). As Maurice Kogan argues in Chapter 1, this is another example of research evidence being ignored because it does not fit the prevailing *zeitgeist*.

The overall pattern emerging from this survey, however, records in detail that skill levels in the British workforce are rising, that most jobs have become more demanding and that training times are lengthening – all providing evidence of the increasing importance of human capital.

These general issues are explored in Chapter 4 by Therese Dowswell and her colleagues in the particular context of 'updating' staff in the National Health Services the UK's largest employer. The level of support from employers for lifelong learning varied, however, so considerably from locality to locality that the researchers concluded that "continuing education is as much a matter of chance as management". Such variation in the financial support for professional development was the main source of resentment among staff, but the increasing emphasis on academic qualifications was also proving contentious because higher qualifications were thought by staff to do little to improve practice although considered valuable in the job market.

Individual responsibility

Therese Dowswell and her colleagues also contend that in the NHS the costs of lifelong learning are not only financial (eg loss of overtime), but psychological, with those staff who have children suffering particularly. The main reason is that the responsibility for continuing education has been transferred from employers to individuals, who are now expected to undertake further training in their own time.

In a similar vein, Will Bartlett and Teresa Rees record in Chapter 6 the breakdown of the traditional progression of a career in hierarchical organisations and the increasing pressure on "individuals to take responsibility for, and to manage their lifetime career, which may involve multiple individual careers".

These moves to treat the individual as one of the main targets of policy began under previous Conservative administrations, but show every sign of intensifying under New Labour. For instance, the Green Paper on lifelong learning, *The Learning Age*, describes the "individual learning revolution" as one in which "individuals and enterprises increasingly take charge of their own learning" (DfEE, 1998a, p 17). And the catalyst which the Green Paper claims will create this learning revolution is a national system of individual learning accounts, the first principle of which is that "individuals are best placed to choose what and how they want to learn" (DfEE, 1998a, p 27). But the evidence emanating from the following chapters and from other projects[4] within *The Learning Society Programme* is that those who currently do not participate in lifelong learning are precisely those who are least able to exercise this responsibility.

Practical recommendations

Will Bartlett and Teresa Rees describe in Chapter 6 how the careers service in Further Education Colleges is minimal in comparison with its well-provided counterpart in the universities. They speculate that the latter could be extended not only to lifelong provision of guidance for all graduates throughout their careers but also to adult non-graduates and the adult guidance sector more generally.

This is but one instance of the many constructive suggestions contained in this volume. One further example will be quoted because Michael Eraut's study of the development of knowledge and skills in the engineering, financial services and healthcare sectors also contains important messages for the government's current drive to engender a culture of professional development among teachers (DfEE, 1998b).

Michael Eraut and his colleagues (in Chapter 2) examined the formal systems of training (eg appraisal, mentoring, personal development plans) and concluded that these deal with only a small part of what is learned at work. Far more significant, but far less visible, were all types of informal learning which were neither specified nor planned, such as consultation and collaboration with colleagues.

Much learning resulted from the challenges posed by work and from social interactions at work with colleagues and customers. Their findings also highlight the role of the manager as staff developer:

> *... the local manager may influence learning more through her or his effect on the micro-climate of the workplace and the organisation of work, and through personal example, than through formally recognised activities such as appraisal or sending people on courses.*

The policy implications of this project underline the need to select and train managers who know how to create micro-climates which promote informal learning and the collective capabilities of their subordinates[5]. In contrast, the government's strategy, explicitly based as it is on a statutory scheme of rigorous annual appraisal and individual targets for teachers, may, for all its rigour and concern for accountability, still miss the most significant features of professional learning in schools.

Into a new future?

The relations between research and policy have always and everywhere been problematical with few successes to boast of, as Maurice Kogan concludes in his overview in the first chapter. We are, however, about to enter a new phase in this relationship with the commitment of the New Labour government to developing "evidence-based policy and practice" (see Clarke, 1998). This change of course is likely to be widely welcomed by the research community because dialogue with government is preferable to talking only to oneself or one's colleagues. For instance, researchers within *The Learning Society Programme* have learned to sharpen their policy recommendations by engaging in dialogue at joint seminars with Department for Education and Employment officials and with members of the House of Commons Select Committee on Education and Employment. Moreover, each project has involved at each stage of its research a wide range of users and beneficiaries, relevant to the central themes under investigation; and four dissemination conferences for these users and beneficiaries have been planned to take place in Glasgow, London, Cardiff and Belfast in 1999.

The terms of engagement between researchers, policy makers and practitioners have yet to be determined and all parties need to be aware of past failures, of present differences and of the changes required on all sides if the chances of future success are to be increased. Many of the past conflicts and present misunderstandings between the three groups can be attributed to the three different cultures or "normative worlds" which they inhabit. Colin Bell and David Raffe (1991) use the term "normative worlds" to represent the different views of research by the three sets of professionals. According to Bell and Raffe, tensions are created because each group has a different definition of what constitutes good and bad research and a different conception of the objectives, appropriate time-scales, and the management and control of research. Three different cultures with conflicting sets of expectations, criteria and requirements are likely to clash, particularly if their differences remain implicit or are only partially understood. In short, the declared intention of government to base policy and practice on research will not eliminate inherent tensions: partnerships provide no panacea.

Indeed, calls for a new partnership are usually employed to disguise a shift in power and the most likely consequence of the new arrangements is an increase in central control, whether overt or covert, over what research is to be funded and published. It is worth exploring the dangers of such an outcome which could result in ministers unintentionally restricting themselves to a bland, fibre-free diet.

First, ministers, policy makers and practitioners understandably require immediate answers to pressing problems, but the time government departments currently allow for the submission of applications and final reports has become so short that careful planning, reflection on findings, and dialogue with fellow experts before publication are perforce skimped or omitted altogether. High quality research is both time-consuming and expensive; and a proper understanding of our national systems of education, training and employment cannot be based on a set of cheaply produced snap-shots.

Second, working conditions for researchers are likely to become more restrictive. If the ordering of priorities, the problems to be tackled and the methods to be employed are all to be decided centrally, then independent researchers will be tempted to behave like hired consultants who serve up what they think their pay-masters want to hear.

Third, the intellectual climate for educational research is likely to deteriorate. At its best, independent, critical research exists to question the taken-for-granted assumptions and practices of practitioners and policy makers, to ask subversive questions, to explore alternative perspectives, to expose the strengths and weaknesses in existing policies, to use new knowledge to articulate different visions of the future, to suggest radical change, to introduce via theory other languages to illuminate enduring problems, and to stick unwelcome findings under the nose of government. *Speaking truth to power*[6] has always been a fraught and risky business from the time of the messenger in Greek tragedy to the present; and educational research will only flourish in a climate:

> *... in which the unthinkable can be thought, in which research and scholarship of a completely non-utilitarian kind can be undertaken and where the search for knowledge can be celebrated as an end in itself. The justification is not simply that such conditions are fundamental to all basic research in science. It is that they are at the root of all creative endeavour in a vibrant culture and civilisation and, in a fundamental way, the source of all thought about the values which ought to govern our lives. (Coffield and Williamson, 1997, p 127)*

It is to be hoped that most ministers and senior civil servants in a democratic society would accept that this general argument applies as much to education as any other discipline. The troubles begin when the researchers' insistence on open-ended inquiry, on the right to question everyone and everything, and on complex understandings of the untidy messes we call educational problems clash with the policy makers' need to make coherent and politically feasible decisions about action, based on clear and manageable data.

The above argument could – with some justice – be criticised as a justification of the status quo and of university-based researchers retaining control over educational research. With characteristic panache and good timing, David Hargreaves has recently argued for a fundamental reconstruction of relations between university researchers, school teachers and policy makers with regard to research on teaching and learning. Briefly, he demonstrates the particular relevance for education of the thesis of Michael Gibbons and colleagues about "the emergence of a new mode of knowledge production" (1994, p 13), which they label Mode 2. Mode 1 represents the institutionalised mode of knowledge production, which is disciplinary, homogenous and hierarchical. By contrast, Mode 2 produces knowledge in the context of application, and is transdisciplinary and heterogeneous: "it is characterised by a constant flow back and forth between the fundamental and the applied, between the theoretical and the practical" (Gibbons et al, 1994, p 19).

It is David Hargreaves' contention that "while some Mode 1 'basic' research should be protected, the pace and scale of the transition to Mode 2 must increase dramatically if government targets for educational improvement are to be met" (1998, p 22). This proposal to transform knowledge-receiving schools into knowledge-creating schools is applauded, but three key difficulties are anticipated. First, as Hargreaves himself recognises, adequate time and resources will have to be found to enable a new cadre of teachers to engage in the continuous negotiations which are such a notable feature of Mode 2.

Second, prioritising research into teaching and learning may lead to an unduly restrictive agenda for educational research, particularly if it neglects larger themes such as the purposes of education, its funding and assessment. If these are the issues Hargreaves wishes to class under 'basic' research, then the distinction between Modes 1 and 2 should be dispensed with because the two sets of issues interact. Indeed, an historical and empirical examination of Gibbons' thesis concludes that Mode 2 is not a new phenomenon and that there have never been two modes of research, but only one – Mode 2. The sociological analysis by Michael Gibbons and his colleagues is best viewed, argues Benoit Godin[7], as a political tract whose main purpose is to criticise academics:

The implications, which some public bodies already draw out explicitly, are that any type of research other than academic research as we know it would be better; that any knowledge – whatever its source – would be as reliable as any other; that all knowledge should be co-produced, and so on. (Godin, 1998, p 479)

Third, such an open-ended strategy will require government to shift from its current centralising tendency, where outcomes are predetermined and prescribed in ever increasing detail, to a decentralising policy of establishing the general conditions within which networks of researchers and practitioners jointly create and disseminate the professional knowledge they need. This imaginative proposal is predicated on radical change in the roles of all the partners, but it will take courageous and atypical politicians to initiate policy which diminishes their own power.

In other words, there is little prospect of developing a learning society in the UK if the government itself does not become a model of learning and of managing change. Government departments, for instance, continue to announce extensions to major initiatives before the evaluation of the pilot projects has even started. More importantly, the commitment to research-based policy and practice needs to be total and not just employed where the balance of evidence fits departmental or ministerial thinking and ignored otherwise. And the democratic process of consultation is debased if only the details but not the principles of radical change are negotiable. Passionate belief – even that of a Secretary of State – is no substitute for evidence.

Whether David Hargreaves' decentralising proposal or the government's more centralising strategy or some compromise between these two approaches is adopted, the roles and practices of both educational researchers and practitioners are likely to be subjected to intensifying pressure to change in the next few years. Change is, however, also required of those politicians and policy makers who are so eager to reform research and practice – above all, a recognition that their shiny, new policies are often part of the problem rather than part of the solution[8].

Notes

[1] The first publication in the series produced by The Policy Press contains articles by Michael Eraut et al (on learning from other people at work), David Ashton (on learning in organisations), Peter Scott and Antje Cockrill (on training in the construction industry in Wales and Germany), Reiner Siebert (on Jobrotation), Kari Hadjivassilliou et al (on Continuous Vocational Training), and Stephen Baron et al (on what the learning society means for adults with learning difficulties).

[2] The second report, entitled *Why's the beer always stronger up North? Studies of lifelong learning in Europe*, contains some cross-national observations on lifelong learning by Walter Heinz (Bremen); an article on adult guidance services in Europe by Teresa Rees and Will Bartlett; a chapter on different models of continuous vocational training in the UK, France and Spain by Isabelle Darmon and colleagues; a comparison of credit-based systems of learning in London and Northern France by Pat Davies; a study of the links between initial and continuing education in Scotland, Northern Ireland and England by Tom Schuller and Andrew Burns; a comparison of policy strategies to reduce the divisions between academic and vocational learning in England and Scotland by David Raffe and colleagues; and, finally, reflections on devising and conducting cross-national studies in the social sciences by Antje Cockrill and colleagues.

[3] The fourth report on *Informal learning* contains chapters by Pat Davies on the formalisation of informal learning via credits; by Stephen Baron and colleagues on the role of implicit knowledge in supported employment for adults with learning difficulties; by John Field on the links between informal learning and social capital; by Ralph Fevre and colleagues on the acquisition of necessary knowledge and skills via informal rather than formal learning; and, finally, by Michael Eraut on how tacit knowledge is acquired in professional work.

[4] See, for example, the conclusion of Gareth Rees, Ralph Fevre and John Furlong (1999) to the effect that "those who failed at school often come to see post-school learning of all kinds as irrelevant to their needs and capacities. Hence, not only is participation in further, higher and continuing

education not perceived to be a realistic possibility, but also work-based learning is viewed as unnecessary".

[5] Informal learning was not the central focus of the work of any of the 14 projects but its significance soon began to be appreciated by a number of project directors. A conference on this theme was held and the papers presented will constitute the fourth report in this series.

[6] Harold Silver (1990, p 17) explains that *Telling truth to power* was the "American title of Aaron Wildavsky's 1979 book, published in Britain under the title *The Art and Craft of Policy Analysis*", in 1980.

[7] Maurice Kogan kindly brought this article to my attention.

[8] I am grateful to the following colleagues for their perceptive comments on an earlier version of this introduction: Stephen Ball, Bruce Carrington, Kathryn Ecclestone, Tony Edwards, Michael Eraut, Alan Felstead and Maurice Kogan.

References

Ball, S.J. (1990) *Politics and policy making in education*, London: Routledge.

Ball, S.J. (1997) 'Policy sociology and critical social research: a personal review of recent education policy and policy research', *British Educational Research Journal*, vol 23, no 3, pp 257-74.

Bell, C. and Raffe, D. (1991) 'Working together? Research, policy and practice', in G. Walford (ed) *Doing educational research*, London: Routledge, pp 121-46.

Clarke, C. (1998) 'Resurrecting research to raise standards', *British Educational Research Association Newsletter*, no 66, August, pp 8-9.

Coffield, F. (ed) (1997) *A national strategy for lifelong learning*, Newcastle: Department of Education, University of Newcastle.

Coffield, F. (1999) *Breaking the consensus: Lifelong learning as social control*, Newcastle: Department of Education, University of Newcastle, Inaugural Lecture, 2 February.

Coffield, F. and Williamson, B. (eds) (1997) *Repositioning higher education*, Buckingham: Open University Press/SRHE.

DfEE (Department for Education and Employment) (1998a) *The Learning Age: A renaissance for a new Britain*, Cm 3790, London: The Stationery Office.

DfEE (1998b) *Teachers: Meeting the challenge of change*, Cm 4164, London: The Stationery Office.

Edwards, A. (1998) 'A careful review but some lost opportunities', *British Educational Research Association Newsletter*, no 66, October, pp 15-16.

Fryer, R.H. (1997) *Learning for the twenty-first century*, London: DfEE.

Gibbons, M., Limoges, C., Nowotny, H., Schwartzman, S., Scott, P. and Trow, M. (1994) *The new production of knowledge: The dynamics of science and research in contemporary societies*, London: Sage Publications.

Godin, B (1998) 'Writing preformative history: the new new Atlantis?', *Social Studies of Science*, vol 28, no 3, June, pp 465-83.

Goldstein, H. (1998) 'Flawed sampling falls down', *Times Educational Supplement*, 9 October, p 25.

Hammersley, M. (1998) 'Who questions the questioners?', *Times Educational Supplement*, October 9, p 25.

Hargreaves, D. (1998) *Creative professionalism: The role of teachers in the knowledge society*, London: Demos.

Hillage, J., Pearson, R., Anderson, A. and Tamkin, P. (1998) *Excellence in research on schools*, Research Report RR 74, London: DfEE.

Nisbet, J. and Broadfoot, P. (1980) *The impact of research on policy and practice in education*, Aberdeen: Aberdeen University Press.

Rees, G., Fevre, R. and Furlong, J. (1999) *End of award report*, Swindon: ESRC.

Silver, H. (1990) *Education, change and the policy press*, London: Falmer Press.

Silver, H. (1999: forthcoming) *Researching education: Themes from teaching-and-learning*, Bristol: The Policy Press.

Steel, J. and Sausman, C. (1997) 'The contribution of graduates to the economy: rates of return', in The National Committee of Inquiry, *Higher education in the learning society* (The Dearing Report), Report 7, pp 83-106.

Tooley, J. and Darby, D. (1998) *Educational research: A critique*, London: OFSTED.

Woodhead, C. (1998) 'Foreword', in J. Tooley and D. Darby, *Educational research: A critique*, London: OFSTED.

The impact of research on policy

Maurice Kogan

Introduction

Research is supposed to be good for us – as Ulrich Teichler (1993) once put it, an aerobic activity. Yet educational and similar social science research, whether concerned with policy or practice issues, has no encouraging history of application. This can be blamed on practitioners and policy makers – if they would only listen – on the lack of relevance or of the communicability of the research, or on the nature of the phenomena being researched. I have conducted research on policy-related issues for about 30 years now, yet in the watches of the night I find it difficult to say how far any of my work or that of my colleagues has contributed to policy.

I will first refer to what we know about its successes and failures in contributing to major policy shifts and the difficulties of using research. I will then consider the characteristics of policy making as a receptor of research and other kinds of knowledge and outline some of the obstacles to application. Then, I discuss the institutional requirements for interaction, and, finally, try to pick out some summary operational points.

Successes and failures

Policy making obviously depends, or should depend, on the use of knowledge. Yet it is rare for policies to start with systematic and rational analysis. They are more likely to be akin to prophesy, usually starting with an exaggerated version of what is going wrong with the world, and then suggesting radical but not well-rooted solutions. Perhaps the Swedes tried

rationality hardest, with their powerful system of royal commissions and Parliamentary committees and by setting up research upon which they could base policy development. That system lasted so long, I am sure, because for a whole generation Sweden was governed by one party, and that party was strong on both democratic and intellectual values. Recently, the Swedish social democratic tradition has been criticised (Åasen, 1993) for its adherence to a linear model which assumed that basic research could lead to applied research, which in its turn could feed into both policy and practice. More interactive and multilevel approaches are now preferred.

In the UK there have been various stabs at introducing more systematic policy analysis systems – for example, Edward Heath set up Programme Analysis Review in the early 1970s – but for the most part the policies do not conform to a knowledge-based model, but to the heroic model which relies on value setters, such as Joseph, Clarke, Baker and Blunkett, who know what they want, and set out to get it without recourse to supporting or opposing evidence. As Eric Forth put it, "we don't need research to tell us what to do, we know that already." And the nuisance from the researchers' point of view is that that is a legitimate point of view in a democracy: election legitimises the weakest and craziest of policy beliefs. They derive from value preferences that can, but need not be, affected by knowledge.

Examples of the direct effects of research on major policy shifts have been rare. The examples of successful impact may yield a generalisation. Let's take the changing fortunes of 11+. As I understand it, selection at the age of 11 was strongly backed by the findings of educational psychology which demonstrated how it was possible to identify the general factor of intelligence, and to isolate it from the social factors that might affect performance. It was therefore safe and ethical to test and divide children at 11. Indeed, it was seen by Cyril Burt as a means of social justice because it could 'rescue' bright children from the working classes. Then both psychologists and sociologists discovered the opposite and were able to point to a whole cluster of factors – parental attitudes as well as socioeconomic factors – which affected performance. This thinking led to a drastic reversal of policy. So research both helped to create a policy and to reverse it. Very good for trade. The next example comes from the Robbins Report (1963) which legitimised the expansion of higher education. It depended on two pieces of research evidence. It demonstrated, by using evidence from Douglas (1964) and others, that able people were leaving school at the age of 15, and thus weakened the assumption that there was a limited pool of ability. It also used research which demonstrated the importance of human capital and the link between educational investment and the economy, on the basis of reports by Bowen, Blaug and others. This contrasted with Dearing's refusal to accept the research evidence, provided by Analytical Services of the Department for Education and Employment (Steel and Sausman, 1997, p 100), that the supply of new graduates already exceeds and will continue to exceed demand.

The generalisation to be drawn from those examples is that it need not be the content of the research, or even its truth, that counts – we have only now begun to return to the human capital position taken up by Robbins, and watch this space for a return to the 11+ – but the *zeitgeist*. If it contradicts the *zeitgeist* it will have a harder time getting through. Each of the examples I have given is of research well matching the intelligent wisdom of its time. Remember that the 11+ was regarded as a progressive and egalitarian device, helping local education authorities to identify able youngsters who hitherto had stood small chance of getting the education they needed, within what Anthony Crosland (1962) called the soft or weak concept of equality. The reversal of these practices would have

matched the more open egalitarianism of the 1960s. If it is wisdom that accords with the views of those currently in power then it will certainly be listened to. Our kind of knowledge is largely indeterminate, unlike clinical research within health studies. If it addresses macro-policies it has to wait for the political agenda to move in its favour. Social and distributive issues are bound to depend on political evaluations for their pursuit in action. So much of the knowledge needed for policy planning is probably taken for granted or generated by government's own staff or derived from what Cohen and Lindblom (1979) call Ordinary Knowledge. That which comes from the research world must either accord with current policy directions or be negotiated with policy makers.

Two examples of the use of knowledge which both confirm and mitigate this picture are studies generated by various think tanks and work that has directly attacked policy agendas. The work of think tanks is primarily that of policy analysis, that is to say, they take largely existing knowledge and reshape it towards meeting problems that are perceived to be on the policy agenda. How far they reflect and how far they help to shape the *zeitgeist* is a matter for contemplation. But it would be fair to say that their influence depends more on their ability to provide alternatives to policies than to create new knowledge deriving from the traditional academic ideal of the disinterested search for truth. A second major example is the influences brought to bear upon current social and employment policies and practices by reflective thinking on gender and ethnic issues. Some of this work is rooted deeply in sociological, psychological, anthropological and legal studies. But it would, again, be fair to say that its initiation, take-off and impact result as much from its connection with the remedy of perceived injustice as to its research qualities and content[1].

Many government departments do have large research programmes. It is their role in policy making that might be questioned. In the 1970s, a lot of hope was invested in them, and programmes were set up on fairly liberal assumptions of researchers' freedom to negotiate the objectives of the research. But these have increasingly been directed to the short-term consultancy needs of policy makers rather than to any intention to analyse social phenomena from first principles.

Indeed, the widespread use of consultants rather than researchers is based on the premise that policy objectives are not to be scrutinised but rather that expertise should be recruited to secure aspects of implementation (Henkel, 1992). That, too, is the kind of knowledge (perhaps it could be called managerial information) that is created by inspection or audit. Increasingly, too, the research councils have been persuaded by a highly directed Office of Science and Technology system into meeting agendas created from outside the research community.

The difficulties of using research

From their perspective it is not easy for policy makers to use research. Here is the judgement of a former Permanent Secretary, "I know of no strategic issue with which Ministers were concerned which was illuminated by the Health Services Research Programme" (Stowe, 1989). One conceptualisation of these difficulties is the empirically-based modelling by Bardach (1984). He assumed individual rationality on the part of policy makers. He showed how research reaches those for whom its utility exceeds the disutility of obtaining it. Cooperative relationships grow up with consumers when producers try to reduce the cost to them of obtaining information. Bardach argued, too, that the natural sciences model of rapid and authoritative dissemination is inappropriate to the social sciences and to professionals. The penetration of the social sciences is 'shallower' than that of the natural sciences. They have difficulty in getting much below the surface of the phenomena they study. More important, "the contextual component of the policy making craft generally far exceeds that of the general principles component" (Bardach, 1984), important in identifying the type of evidence associated with good uptake.

We must certainly not put everything down to original sin. Policy making has different knowledge concerns from those of research. The word decision means to cut away from. Policy making involves the reduction of pressures from interests so as to make them manageable. By contrast, research opens things up by questioning existing states, or their consequences. Policy makers have to get and keep things working; researchers have legitimacy to

question, test and criticise. There is a necessary tension, and sometimes it seems an unbridgeable gap, between policy and research, because they represent "two different cultures with different requirements" (Levin, 1991).

The other reasons for the lack of impact take me a bit outside my remit, but it has been noted that in most cases the officials commissioning the research have moved on, and there is no continuity of reception of the findings of research that they had commissioned; evaluative schemes have been poorly conceptualised; there are conflicting policies and 'tribalism' at work within single government departments (Kogan and Henkel, 1983). Yet in the attempt in the 1980s to install the Rothschild customer–contractor system, it was seen as possible to get scientists and policy makers together (in research liaison groups), to make a study of the current pattern of research, the gaps in research that are required for practice and policy, and to commission work directed to filling the gaps. Eventually it failed because of the opposition of the medical establishment. They believed that research should be guided primarily by scientific or curiosity imperatives, or medical need as perceived by clinicians, rather than by the perceptions of health needs generated by policy makers. Such an experiment has never been tried in education.

The heroic model applies to major policy shifts – creating and sustaining OFSTED, students' fees, comprehensive schools, and so on. There are also much slower processes of policy accretion and clarification. These might emerge from continuing contact with the professional, with client groups and governing infrastructures rather than political ambition. Again, they need not depend on research, but do depend on a relatively open and learning style of government.

Evidence of payback

This pessimistic account of the policy–practice–research relationship is somewhat mitigated by the work of two colleagues (Buxton and Hanney, 1994) working in the fields of health and social services. They identified payback from research from a study of eight cases ranging from heart transplants to social care management. They concluded that a number of the studies appeared to have had a direct and significant impact on policy and executive decisions, for example, in care management legislation and funding of heart transplants. Other studies became part of a body of evidence that led to clinical guidance. But the case studies also identified research that was largely ignored in the policy debate. The list of factors identified as being associated with high payback emphasised the importance of recruiting and maintaining user interest. They included: continuing support from customers; liaison with stakeholders; appropriateness and quality of research; brokerage; appropriate disseminations, ongoing programmes in their own right and as a context for specific projects. I suggest that some of these conditions are not to be found in the current conditions of short order commissioning that we now enjoy. And also note that these conditions of interaction are not at all the conditions we would seek for fundamental, independent research.

Away from the linear model

The crisis of confidence in education research was caused in part by an overselling of the researchers' products (Husén, 1989). This was associated with the belief of researchers, but also many policy makers, in the 1960s and 1970s, in a linear relationship between quantitative research, reform planning, and improved practice (Åasen, 1993). Work conducted by policy analysts later discredited this perspective (Nisbet and Broadfoot, 1980; Weiss, 1982, 1989; Husén, 1989). As a recent OECD report (1993) suggests: "The view most widely held today is that the linear model of research utilisation is fundamentally flawed, and that educational research findings can only very seldomly be applied directly in practice."

The linear model is one among many models of interaction (Buxton and Hanney, 1994). I can only briefly enumerate them here: the classic, purist, knowledge-driven model, which is the linear model to which I have already referred; the problem-solving engineering model, also linear, but beginning with a problem to be solved. This underlaid the Rothschild Report proposals for the customer–contractor relationship; the political model in which research is used to back or refute a

political argument; the enlightenment, percolative or limestone model; and the interactive, social interaction model. In this latter case, the research process itself interacts with the policy process in determining objectives and the use made of outcomes.

Opposition to the linear and utilitarian perspective mounted during the 1970s, when researchers increasingly turned to 'qualitative' or 'interpretative' methods. Action research, ethnography, discourse analysis and other hermeneutical and phenomenological approaches to policy research became increasingly popular among a growing number of researchers, who did not share the basic tenets of the functionalist interpretation of the relationship between educational research and decision making.

During the 1980s, once the inadequacy of the linear model of research and development had been established, the debate gradually shifted to the ways in which the potential contribution of research could be realised. It is in application to teaching and learning that policy makers still feel the strongest lack in the knowledge base provided to them (OECD, 1993). Luckily for me, the question of how far research is useful to classroom practice is outside my competence. I have, however, recently heard two professors of education – one British and the other Austrian – say that there is a science of education which can show teachers how to produce better results. Pity the rest of world knows so little about this. I do know that a study by Benjamin Bloom in the 1940s analysed 70,000 pieces of education research and found that only 70 had any likely use in practical application. I would be more confident of statements to the effect that good research may sharpen teachers' awareness of the factors and contexts that affect teaching and learning, and that it may contribute to helpful self-interrogation.

While research can have instrumental effects, directly influencing decisions, if it has effects at all, more often it shapes policy maker perceptions and agendas, as in Carol Weiss' notion of enlightenment (Weiss, 1980). Meta analysis can lead to 'short order' analyses which might contribute to immediate policy concerns as well as give pointers for worthwhile further studies. Researchers can certainly apply research techniques to evaluative studies. They are less certain about their ability to demonstrate to government what works best. Their key function is to raise issues and questions and to test from an independent standpoint received policy and practice wisdoms.

Hypotheses for further research may be derived from single case studies conducted in the field of education, but firm propositions, let alone scientific principles or laws, cannot be derived in this way. Meta-evidence emanating from many studies and research replicated over time, under different conditions and employing different designs and methods, is required in establishing propositions and principles for policy and practice. That would be difficult work requiring sustained investment in research (OECD, 1995).

Researchers face the problem that the potency of a statement in our field need not depend on the rigour with which it is formulated. Take, for example, that for most of the time the press and politicians will say that standards in schools are dropping. That fact is testable empirically by processes that first set up criteria of success or failure, determine the extent to which the criteria are to be subject to normative adjustment according to contexts, and then go in and measure on some time series. But even if not proven in that way, the statement takes on a truth quality by virtue of the fact that it is widely believed and thus conditions political actions. It becomes what Cohen and Lindblom (1979) call Ordinary Knowledge, which is then converted into Usable Knowledge. The social scientist attempting to evaluate standards may then have to take it as datum that there is popular belief that standards are dropping because the belief in itself affects teacher behaviour and their expectations of pupils. Standards may thus be affected by it. It is like the 'unreal' market in economics where sentiment in the City will affect the price of stock and the exchange rates despite what might be happening to production or exports.

So there are severe epistemological and operational problems in connecting policy and research. To go back to one example, the policy maker is more likely to be interested in *how* standards can be raised rather than whether they have fallen or risen. The recent OECD report (1995) recited some other more mundane reasons concerning funding, training and organisation on both sides of the divide.

Policy needs

Granted that it is all too difficult, what is the kind of knowledge needed by policy makers? There are several levels of knowledge which are relevant. They are: knowledge directly relevant to macro-decisions, on the overall objectives and structure of the system; and knowledge concerning the processes and outcomes of work at the practitioner level. In between, there are several intermediate kinds of knowledge, for example, about the ways in which local authorities or governing bodies work. We could add to these concerns evaluation of the efficacy of government. We have had enormous changes in the whole orientation of policy and in the mechanisms for carrying it out. But neither government itself nor the major central evaluative bodies such as the National Audit Office have asked such questions as: How far do its objectives meet the real needs of the economy and society? How far is it capable of knowing enough to do its job properly? What is the cost of implementing reforms? How does the knowledge created by OFSTED or funding councils enter the policy blood stream?

At the same time, what is missing in national policy making is what Martin Rein (1973) called 'hot knowledge', the developing knowledge generated by professional practitioners who have to 'deliver' the curriculum, who face the client groups and whose vision of reality may be quite different from that of the central curriculum makers and inspectors. Hot knowledge grows cold when far away from its point of origin. For it to have an impact on policy the contacts between the producers of the knowledge and policy makers have to be close and continuous.

The knowledge which takes pride of place in official thinking is quite cold. Central administrators have to decontextualise if they are to make overarching judgements. The legitimacy of overarching judgements, in comparison with those of the field professionals, becomes weaker the nearer one gets to action.

Links between policy and *The Learning Society Programme*

So far I have said little about research that deals with the micro-issues. Here I can do no better than briefly locate the kind of research promoted in *The Learning Society Programme* within my frame of reference which is the relationship between research and policy making.

Each of the projects has made a stab at suggesting what policy implications their research will offer. Many of the hoped-for outcomes should be self-evidently relevant to policy making at the national level. For example, determining what factors are decisive in the educational choices made by students and parents should enable policy makers to consider how they and providers might affect the market for courses and other options within which students must operate. Or determining the best practice in guidance services could be the focus of national guidance policy. Other studies, such as the Learning Society's Exeter study of core skills, should interrogate institutional and academic practice, though changing the deep culture of higher education is no easy task, as the Enterprise Initiative, surely the most ambitious project of all, showed.

So these projects – I won't mention them all – are potentially full of issues that ought to influence policy and practice, and I would like to see their ultimate impact evaluated. I said before, however, that it is not the truth or quality of research that gives hope of policy take-up so much as the appeal of the issue to the political *zeitgeist* of the time. The Learning Society is certainly part of the official rhetoric, and we might hope that one of the conditions for payback – that the objectives of this programme have been worked out in collaboration with policy makers – has been met. The other factors enhancing impact will involve liaison and negotiation with stakeholders, brokerage, appropriate dissemination and follow-up programmes.

What might be the links between micro-research and policy formations? I have already referred to the need for hot knowledge to have its place in the hierarchy of knowledge which is put to use. It is worrying that policy makers who used to be informed – not well enough and somewhat unsystematically – of what was going on in the field and therefore the impact of their policies, by Her Majesty's Inspectors of Schools (HMIs), and by constant contact with the major local authority and teacher interest groups, are now virtually cut off from that kind of hands-on knowledge. Much knowledge comes instead through OFSTED or Funding Council evaluations or inspections, but that is hardly free rein knowledge. It is concerned with assessing performance against severely prestructured criteria, and its function is corrective or allocative rather than exploratory or developmental. It is hardly the kind of exercise that assumes that life is and should be full of surprises and that we are dealing with a world which is constantly moving and being shaped by the teachers and pupils who are actors within it. I am not clear how far the Training and Enterprise Councils and regional government offices are a source of hot knowledge for policy making.

But the perceptions and modelling of particular aspects of a policy that come from research should be particularly valuable to policy makers because it is precisely the kind of knowledge of what is happening, working or not working, that they are unlikely to get in any other way. The problem will be that raised by Bardach – the difficulty of getting away from immediate contexts, so that generally applicable principles can be exploited. At minimum, particular researchers should feed the policy makers' thinking, and raise questions for them, even if they do not provide overarching generalisations on which large-scale policies can be based. Large-scale policies could be assessed, for example, such as current policies for lifelong learning.

Supporting a wide range of disciplined enquiry

Finally, I turn to some of the institutional aspects of policy-useful research. Policy-related studies allow for a wide range of knowledge generation and use and go well beyond the normal definition of research – the discovery of new knowledge. What Cronbach and Suppes (1969) have called 'disciplined enquiry' encompasses research, development, scholarship, applied research, consultancy and evaluative studies. Each mode can be used opportunistically as long as they are made credible by conforming to the academic criteria of evidence, logic and demonstrability.

If, however, education depends substantially on consultancy, or inspection and audit, for its knowledge without the testing and refreshment of concepts provided by curiosity driven research, in the end it will be banal and purvey no more than received wisdom. Equally, if theory and scholarship are not recurrently tested by the shifting experience of education at all its levels, it will be abstract and devoid of relevant content. The different forms of knowledge should form a virtuous cycle in which critique ultimately strengthens operational knowledge. Good 'real' research will illuminate either critically or supportively the actions of the activists. Only weak development eschews critical evaluation. The system needs those able to bring together knowledge of how best to provide staff development, ensure competent and fair evaluation and install good systems of management and administration. Those undertaking these tasks do best if they have a firm grasp of changes in the theories of knowledge and curriculum structure; of evaluative theory and the enormous ambiguities and ambivalences that evaluation produces, as well as the research-based technical issues of how to ensure validity and reliability. Management structures are saturated by problems which are the bread and meat of political science and organisational sociology.

This implies open and eclectic forms of organisation and sponsorship. Public policy research cannot do without public funds. But there is always the question of who will set the agenda. In giving contracts for sectoral research there are good examples of governments that take care to work out collaboratively the objectives of the research and its mode of operation. They may also be liberal in their policies on publication. But there are many unsatisfactory aspects of research commissioning in many countries. We are experiencing immature customers everywhere. They may know what they want, but do not negotiate the objectives of the work. They ask for tenders at very short notice – sometimes a few weeks for work to be started in a few weeks and to completed without a period of reflection on what all this new knowledge may mean for policy. The balance of funding has shifted seriously from independent research to consultancy and sectoral research.

Given adequate support, financial, institutional and political, there is room for mutuality between the world of policy and action and that of academic exploration. This requires a good structure for research commissioning in which there is a reasonable balance struck between mission-oriented and curiosity-driven forms of enquiry and active responsiveness to clients at all levels. Government machinery must ensure that research and development is well related to the products of evaluation, and that users' as well as providers' perspectives are recruited to the commissioning processes. Thought must also be given to ways of sustaining the research community through adequate training and career progression. Government needs to give some thought to developing a supply chain of able researchers in the way that Nissan does for motor manufacture. This will be all the more important as the economy continues to open up and good alternative employment will present itself.

Some operational conclusions

By way of summary, let me note what might be the constituents of a model for relating policy and research:

- Some research, that mainly of a descriptive analytic type, is essential to policy makers. The compositions of education populations, social distributions and the like are obvious examples. Much of the evaluative data now being collated by OFSTED are also examples.

- Other research that could directly assist policy making presents difficulties of aggregation and generalisation. That points for a need for far more scholarship – the collation and reconceptualisation of existing knowledge – than is usually allowed for.

- Yet other research opens up fields of enquiry and uncertainty rather than helps policy makers reach clear conclusions. But if the uncertainty reflects the reality, the able policy maker should use it to contribute to the continuing policy agenda and also to help them look out for the unintended consequences of policy making.

- For basic and independent research, relationships between policy makers and researchers need to be developed cautiously, if at all. But where the research is intended to be directly useful there can be negotiation over its objectives and some collaboration on interpreting the results. In this the researchers and policy makers might include several stakeholders, including clients.

- The value of research to practitioners may be multiple. It is a means of creating a self-interrogatory ethos which may help the teaching profession improve their knowledge base and self-perception as professionals, and be more effective in challenging the major official orthodoxies promoted by government.

Note

[1] These points derive from criticisms made of this paper at the Bristol seminar. It was pointed out that the paper was mainly concerned with the impact of research on official policy making and did not pay sufficient attention to other modes of knowledge generation.

References

Åasen, P. (1993) 'Evaluation of Swedish educational R&D', *Research Programme 1992-1995/6*, Stockholm: National Agency for Education.

Bardach, E. (1984) 'The dissemination of policy research to policymakers', *Knowledge*, vol 6, no 2, December.

Buxton, M. and Hanney, S. (1994) *Assessing payback from Department of Health research and development*, Preliminary Report, vol 1, *The Main Report*, Health Economics Research Group, Brunel University.

Cohen, D. and Lindblom, C.E. (1979) *Usable knowledge*, New Haven, CT: Yale University Press.

Cronbach, L. and Suppes, P. (eds) (1969) *Research for tomorrow's school. A disciplined enquiry for education*, London: Macmillan.

Crosland, A. (1962) *The conservative enemy*, London: Cape.

Douglas, J.W.B. (1964) *The home and the school. A study of ability and attainment in the primary schools*, London: MacGibbon and Kee.

Henkel, M. (1992) *Government, evaluation and change*, London: Jessica Kingsley Publishers.

Husén, T. (1989) 'Educational research at the crossroads?', *Prospects*, vol 19, no 3, pp 351-60.

Kogan, M. and Henkel, M. (1983) *Government and research*, London: Heinemann Educational Books.

Levin, H.M. (1991) 'Why isn't educational research more useful?', in D.S. Anderson and B.J. Biddle (eds) *Knowledge for policy. Improving education through research*, London: Falmer Press.

Nisbet, J. and Broadfoot, P. (1980) *The impact of research on policy and practice in education*, Aberdeen: Aberdeen University Press.

OECD (1993) Proceedings of the Second OECD-CERI International Seminar on Educational Research and Development, Sunne, Sweden, 25-28 May.

OECD (1995) *Education research and development. Trends, issues and challenges*, Paris: OECD.

Rein, M. (1973) *From policy to practice*, London: Macmillan.

Robbins Report (1963) *Higher education*, Cmnd 2154, London: HMSO.

Steel, J. and Sausman, C. (1997) 'The contribution of graduates to the economy: rates of return', in National Committee of Inquiry into Higher Education, *Higher education in the learning society* (Dearing Report), Report 7, pp 83-106.

Stowe, K. (1989) *On caring for the national health*, London: Nuffield Provincial Hospital Trust.

Teichler, U. (1993) 'Research on higher education in Europe: some aspects of recent developments', in EAIR, *Towards excellence in European higher education in the 1990s*, Proceedings, 11th European AIR Forum, Trier.

Weiss, C. (1980) *Social science research and decision-making*, New York, NY: Columbia University Press.

Weiss, C. (1982) 'Policy research in the context of diffuse decision-making', in G. Kosse (ed) *Social science research and public policy-making*, London: NFER-Nelson.

Weiss, C. (1989) 'Congressional committees as users of analysis', *Journal of Policy Analysis and Management*, vol 8, no 3, pp 411-31.

2

The impact of the manager on learning in the workplace

Michael Eraut, Jane Alderton, Gerald Cole and Peter Senker

Introduction

The Sussex contribution to *The Learning Society Programme* focused on the development of knowledge and skills in employment (Eraut et al, 1998a). Briefly, our study involved double interviews, six to 12 months apart, with 120 people operating at a professional, management or technician level in 12 organisations. These organisations were in the engineering, financial services and healthcare sectors. The approach adopted was that of finding out what kinds of work activity our respondents were currently conducting, what kinds of knowledge and skill were entailed, how they had acquired the capability to do what they now did, and what factors had affected this learning process. Our findings showed that:

- Formal education and training provide only a small part of what is learned at work. Indeed, most of the learning described in our interviews was non-formal, neither clearly specified nor planned. It arose naturally out of the demands and challenges of work-solving problems, improving quality and/or productivity, or coping with change – and out of social interactions in the workplace with colleagues, customers or clients. Responding to such challenges entails both working and learning – one cannot be separated from the other. In retrospect it may be described as *learning from experience*. Although this leads to the development of knowledge, skills and understanding, such learning is often difficult to explain to others.

- Much learning at work derives its purpose and direction from the goals of the work. Achieving the goals often requires learning which is normally accomplished by a combination of thinking, trying things out and talking to other people. Sometimes, however, people recognise a need for some additional knowledge or skill that seems essential for improving the quality of their work, expanding its range or taking on new duties. Learning goals are identified which they pursue by a combination of self-directed learning and taking advantage of relevant learning opportunities as and when they appear. This sometimes involves undertaking some formal training, but almost always requires learning from experience and from other people at work.

- Learning from other people (Eraut et al, 1998b) is sometimes facilitated by organised learning support, which may be formally decided by central policy or informally arranged at local level. The former includes apprenticeships and trainee schemes; while mentoring, shadowing or coaching is more likely to be locally arranged, and generally more effective when it is. The most common form of learning from other people takes the form of consultation and collaboration within the immediate working group: this may include team work, ongoing mutual consultation and support or observation of others in action. Then beyond the immediate work environment, people seek information and advice, often on a reciprocal basis, from other wider professional networks. Only a minority of our respondents made frequent use of written or audio-visual materials like manuals, videos or computer-based training. The rest tried to circumvent materials by getting the information they needed from other people.

- Working for qualifications and short training courses are important for some people at particular stages in their career. Initial training was generally judged better when it was both broad in scope and involved periods in the workplace as well as in the classroom, laboratory or workshop. Mid-career management and professional qualifications were judged highly effective because they were able to use and build on prior experience at work; and management courses involving small groups and projects played an important role in helping people shift their thinking from an operational to a strategic level. What is less recognised, however, is the importance of less visible, work-based learning in developing the capability to use what has been learned off-the-job in work situations. This is especially true for short courses, which have very little impact unless they are appropriately timed and properly followed up at work.

- Increasing the amount of learning at work in order to realise the aspiration conveyed by the rhetoric of the *learning organisation* or *The Learning Society* depends on recognising how much learning occurs, or could occur on the job, and the factors which affect it. Our analysis at the individual level suggests that learning depends on confidence, motivation and capability – especially when capability is viewed as something to be acquired rather than something innate. This in turn depends on people's work having the appropriate degree of challenge, on how they are managed and on the microculture of the immediate work environment. The key person is the local manager whose management of people and role in establishing a climate favourable to learning, in which people seek advice and help each other learn quite naturally, is critical for those who are managed.

These findings have clear significance for the role of the manager, indicating that even the relatively novel concept of *the manager as staff developer* – novel, that is, to most managers – is too narrow. The Human Resource Management literature discusses managers as appraisers, mentors and even coaches. They assess the needs of those they manage,

preferably in collaboration with them, and jointly prepare personal development plans. While the range of methods for supporting learning has widened, the underpinning concept is still based on learning goals being clearly specified and learning opportunities being planned. We found examples of this in our research. But we also found that much learning was neither clearly specified nor planned; indeed it was not easily separated out from the flux of daily living and working. For many people, learning arose out of the challenges posed by their work (McCauley et al, 1994) and out of social interactions in the workplace. The most important factors, apart from the characteristics of the learners themselves, were the nature of the work, the way it was organised and managed, the climate of the immediate workplace and the culture of the organisation (Dubin, 1990). The local manager may influence learning more through their effect on the micro-climate of the workplace and the organisation of work, and through personal example, than through formally recognised activities such as appraisal or sending people on courses.

Each of our respondents worked in unique situations, and the complex array of factors affecting learning could not possibly be subjected to any conclusive quantitative analysis. However, we did seek to collect evidence of how managers affected our respondents and how many of our respondents in their supervisory roles sought to facilitate the learning of those whom they supervised. This evidence is presented here, so that it can be set alongside our earlier findings about respondents' formal and informal learning (Eraut et al, 1998a), to assess how managers affect learning in the workplace. The evidence will be presented in three parts. The first will briefly describe organisational policies which impact upon learning in the workplace. These include: short/long courses, external or in-house; apprenticeship/trainee schemes, induction and rotation; and appraisal systems which range from a relatively informal annual interview to what is now being called performance management. The second will describe activities associated with the concept of the manager as staff developer: appraisal, mentoring and coaching, and other forms of planned learning support. The third will discuss the more informal influence of managers: the manager as role model, positive or negative; the manager as expert, leading professional or strategist; and the influence of managers' informal and incidental behaviour on the micro-climate of the immediate workplace. Overlaps and links between these different types of evidence will be discussed in the conclusion.

Organisational policies

From a manager's perspective organisational policies can appear as dominant, enabling or disinterested. Taking courses as an example, centralised provision of in-house or bought-in courses is quite common. Such policies may be guided by perceptions of organisational weaknesses, strategies for building up particular future capabilities, the need for technical or legal updating, ongoing programmes of skill-formation and management development. Whether or not middle managers are consulted, there is an assumption of needs being similar across the organisation which is sometimes true and sometimes false. More problematic is the difficulty inherent in a central system of timing courses appropriately. Our evidence suggests that timing is often a critical feature in learning from courses. In particular, courses need to relate to participants' current concerns, whether they are present or future orientated. The advantages of central provision, not always realised in practice, are economies of scale, relevance for the organisation and control over the quality of provision. But economies of scale may be counterbalanced by diversity of need; and relevance is difficult to achieve in fast-changing situations. Enabling strategies provide support in the form of funds and advice, to managers seeking to meet the needs of their subordinates or directly to individual employees. In either case the initiative is more likely to come from the employee, and with it more motivation and commitment. The manager's role is to ensure relevance to needs which have been properly assessed and discussed; but with some managers this degenerates to laissez-faire. There is also a danger under either dominant or enabling regimes that too much emphasis is given to courses.

"The company thinks the only solution to learning is training courses rather than other types of experience or other methods." (Engineer)

Apprenticeship/trainee schemes are based on a variety of assumptions. There may be a set of planned learning outcomes, provided by off-the-job training (usually linked to qualifications), structured on-the-job training, or both. This planned learning will usually have a technical emphasis, and was regarded as providing a thorough technical grounding by *all* respondents who had experienced them. A second purpose, usually pursued by a system of rotations, was to acquire knowledge of the organisation. At its simplest, this provides some idea of what the organisation does, but it can also help employees to develop a network of contacts across the organisation who can be consulted later if it should prove necessary. This is more likely to happen where apprentices or trainees are welcomed and supported rather than just tolerated; and this in turn may be influenced by the length of rotations and the number of people being rotated. Apart from one management trainee in a bank and two actuarial trainees in insurance, all the examples encountered were in engineering. However, there are analogies in the placement arrangements for students taking initial and advanced/specialist qualifications in the health professions, particularly radiography. A third purpose, particularly relevant for graduates or qualified technicians, could be the development of a more holistic and strategic view of how the organisation works. One graduate engineering trainee was trying to achieve this, but finding it rather difficult in a relatively small company:

"I filled out the training form and I talked to the manager about it, and he sort of agrees that I would be able to have secondment/shadowing to other departments. I think I wrote four or five down, one I've already been to; and marketing would hopefully be about a four-week secondment; whereas the others would most likely be a week, a couple of days, just shadowing, just to give you a general picture.... But there is a difference between being supportive and actually doing it; 'cause obviously, the longer you're there the more valuable p'raps you become, and you get really involved in the project, and they can't afford [to be without you]."

We did not encounter any other examples of this acquisition of a general view being planned, but there were sufficient examples of people gaining a range of experience across the organisation and clearly benefiting from their consequent increase in organisational understanding for it to be worthy of mention:

> "You need to know about the company…. I've actually worked with an awful lot of departments within the company, and that's helped – … so I actually know what goes on in customer services … the central accounts office … I know what happens in the retail industry, because I've actually worked there…. If you came straight in from outside, you couldn't do the job of corporate hospitality." (PR Manager, Public Utility)

Perhaps this should be conceived more in terms of job rotation during a person's early years in the organisation than as part of a post-entry training scheme.

All four financial organisations had performance management systems (Bevan et al, 1992), but these differed according to:

- frequency of formal meetings
- approaches to performance criteria and target setting
- use of generic skills and competencies
- linkage to pay
- balance between performance evaluation and personal development.

These are illustrated by the following examples from our interviews.

Example 1: insurance manager

"They have a progress review three times a year and an annual review…. So there's a lot of documentation on the person. You've got their file, you can see where they've developed, what their areas of strength and weakness are…. You may already have some personal experience of their strengths and weaknesses … you can start to pick up on those issues, and by observing how their teams run, how they interact with their team, you can see what the morale and issues with the team are…. We are very short-term. We may have one person who's very good at a particular job and we need them to do that job to keep us within target of our performance, so a manager focused on the short term would do that. When that person leaves, gets knocked over by a bus, has two weeks holiday, whatever they do, then suddenly the performance drops. Now what we should be doing and what we haven't done in the past is push those skills throughout the team, take aside three or four people who can do that, let's develop those people, let's develop that person as a trainer even and say, you push those skills through the organisation…. The other thing we do that frustrates me is that that person will then become so expert, that when they want to move on, the manager says, 'I can't lose them, I don't want them to go, it's six months before I can let them go'. That individual is then stopped from all the potential benefits they could bring to the company and themselves by moving on and developing and imparting their knowledge elsewhere, simply because of a process need within one area. That is where I butted up against the culture very heavily … and that is not something I can compromise on."

Example 2: senior sales manager in a bank

"I sign an annual contract at the beginning of the year and again that's based on numbers and performance, income and business objectives, so I get paid on the basis of an annual contract…. Either you meet contract, you exceed contract or you fall short…. As far as fall short is concerned I've given a 'fall short contract' to a manager who works for me and it didn't sit very easily with me, I didn't like doing it but it had to be done, it was the right thing to do. That person is still with us and the way that I tried to deal with it was to turn it on its head and to look at those things that that person could change or influence to make sure that he certainly got a 'met contract' next time round. But I think that if you then get a succession of fall short contracts, your career must be in question: that's not coming from the centre, that's my own personal view."

Example 3: **area manager for a bank**

"We're working with a new system here, a performance management system.... [It] starts off with business goals and takes it through to a personal development plan all in one document.... It's a system we really like but we're still learning it.... It's got a framework, a menu of attributes. So everybody picks out the ones they think are most relevant to their job and then assesses where they are on a level of one to four against definitions that we've got; and then the development plan should fall out of that. So it's much more personal than results focused, although that's in it as well."

Example 4: **finance manager, energy supply company**

"These performance reviews tend not to be looking back, the emphasis is to look forward. They have some key skills, and you actually write down whether each skill is critical for the job, or important, or just nice to have. Then between yourself and your manager you decide where on each scale you ought to be, and then where on the scale you feel you are. If there's a gap, perhaps you need a little bit of training in that area; and then you decide between you and the personnel department what sort of training would be required.... They're trying to make sure that performance reviews are not occasions where you say 'Well, you haven't done very good in that this year', and start beating them around the head. It's meant to be a more positive approach. What can we do to help you become that much better in your job; and if you're quite satisfactory, what can we do to help you go still further? That's only just started, so let's see how it actually works, and whether the staff actually buy into it; 'cause apparently they've had fits and starts on appraisal systems and reviews, they've got a bit of a credibility problem."

Example 5: **accounts manager, energy supply company**

"Our sector's very difficult, because we're split into areas. Some areas are harder to work in than others ... so we have a team target.... We all do equal amounts of work, we're all individually responsible for our own accounts regardless, but at the end of the day all of the figures are lumped together as a team target ... and that forms part of our performance review."

These examples indicate both the range of formal systems, and the ways in which individual managers try and interpret them in ways which match their own personal philosophies of management. They also demonstrate the tension between *performance management systems*, which focus on short-term results and key activities which directly affect 'the bottom line', and a *human resource development* approach focused on the development of staff capability over a longer time-scale (Bevan and Hayday, 1994; Armstrong and Baron, 1998). Reconciling these two approaches depends on the skills of the manager, as discussed in the next two sections. But even the most skilful manager will be constrained (a) when stakes are high because of possible promotions or contingent financial benefits; and (b) when their authority to make

developmental responses to employees' learning needs is limited by finance and/or flexibility.

Performance management systems were not encountered in the engineering and healthcare sectors; but most organisations had a policy of annual appraisals. However, this did not always appear to be taken very seriously or to have been implemented in every department. One important limitation in engineering was the danger of those people who stood to benefit most from appraisal slipping through the net. Those who move departments frequently may leave one department just before they would have been appraised, and arrive at the next one just after appraisals have been completed. A proportion of such people may be having serious career/learning problems which express themselves in frequent moves: it can happen that somebody in particular need of reviewing their career progress and learning misses appraisals for several years running. Nevertheless, many organisations had made recent improvements or were currently working on their implementation:

"There's a formal process in place by which you have to sit down and do this once a year informally and record it, it's a two-way thing between the employee and their immediate manager. I think some people should do it progressively during the course of the year but the mechanism is for making sure once a year you both sit down and actually record it. You can do it as many times as you want, it's really something that you should be working out together. So the company put quite a lot of effort into that, on the flip side because when they first introduced this it wasn't particularly successful. They had quite a long look at it, we had some consultants in; and it was identified that part of the reason for it not working was really the background of the managers. Like myself a lot of the managers were good at doing their previous job, so people assumed they'd be good at being managers; and they put engineers into managerial positions. And there wasn't a lot of support or help given to them in terms of development. So you had an organisation where there were an awful lot of technically competent people; but they were in managerial positions and they were not as confident in terms of doing the managerial bit. So there's been a lot of effort gone into really the managerial side over the last 18 months or so. Most of the managers have gone through the workshop where they sat down in small workshops and tried to work through their various strengths and weaknesses, areas where they need development..." (Manager, engineering company)

"I work with the coaches when we've been developing the performance management systems for each area ... we haven't got many people with those skills to do the job because we have been brought up on good old command and control and tell [whereas] a coach is about enthusing you and encouraging you." (Senior Manager, insurance company)

The manager as staff developer

The best indicator of whether a developmental approach is used by managers will probably be how they manage formal appraisal, informal feedback, and support for learning. These are the central features of 'the manager as staff developer' approach. In this section we summarise our respondents' experiences of appraisal, coaching and general support for learning.

Engineers in product development companies tended to be a little sceptical about appraisal. This may have been because managers, as suggested above, were not well trained in appraisal skills. But it also arises from the limited significance of the line management role when most work is done by project teams. Appraisal can play a useful part in reviewing an engineer's contribution in fairly general terms, both retrospectively and prospectively, but it may not have much impact on learning if the engineer's manager was not involved in any of their projects. Two relatively positive examples are given below, one at the level of general communication, the other giving useful feedback.

"Appraisal is a lot better than it has been, it's something the company have taken more seriously over the last few years.... It certainly lets me have a good feel for the major project that I'll be doing throughout the year.... They look at what you're meant to have done last year, what you actually did last year, why they bear no resemblance, and whether that was your fault or their fault, and then you look at what you will be doing over the next year and how realistic that's likely to be." [Interviewer's probes about learning from appraisal yielded little response] (Manager, engineering company)

"My current manager I think has been very fair. He's given a very good assessment synopsis of where I'm at and I think it will help, definitely, I mean, it focuses on strengths and weaknesses, which I think is important, because, you know, on the one hand you're told what you're good at, but on the other hand you're told what you can do better and what you can develop, improve on, and I think that's useful. You need to have feedback from both sides." (Engineer)

Others commented that their appraisers did little more than discuss possible short courses.

The most interesting example came from a relatively senior manager in an insurance company who was trying to make the appraisal system work in the way it should, by changing managers' attitudes towards feedback from below.

"For my annual review I said to all my team: 'I've got my annual review in a month's time, can you pull together some feedback; and if my boss asks for it, give it to him'. I called him up on the E-mail and said 'Look, if you want some info for my appraisal, here it is'. He never asked for it, so they gave it to him anyway! They said: 'You haven't asked for it but here it is'. I was really pleased, 360° (collecting comments from seniors, juniors and colleagues at the same level) or whatever is not formally part of our appraisal process, but if you seek it and get it back, then you've got something in there that can be used. So we encourage it, and now, my team do it to their people. We are still a bit 'good news-ish', whereas my team go and bring informative stuff, their team didn't give them informative stuff so this honesty thing is probably not quite there yet. When I got the team back for their reviews I said 'Well you're good at everything and bad at nothing. You know what areas you need to develop here'; and they said 'We'll, try to get them to be more open and honest'. But they're not there yet, not that confident with it yet, but they will get there." (Senior Manager, insurance company)

Radiographers missed out on formal appraisal but received a great deal of informal feedback from colleagues. Nurses, being more numerous, tended to be involved in hospital schemes from an early stage. They tended to focus more on the informal activities of their managers than formal appraisals, but there were some positive examples which significantly affected individual careers.

"The actual turning point was when my manager said to me, it was in an appraisal with him, he said 'Right, what are you going to do with the rest of your life? You've got a career. Like it or not you're a career nurse, you've been in it long enough'. I said 'Well I haven't really thought about it', and he said 'Well I think you really need to seriously think about doing your conversion course'. I actually said to him 'Oh I don't think I could do that, you know what do I want to do that for?'; and he said 'I think you've really got to realise that the enrolled nurses are going to be phased out. Your role will be eroded in one way or another'. It really made me think, and I just decided that I'd better go and do the O-levels then. I must admit I loved doing it at night school, I really enjoyed it." [This led to two years' night school, then a conversion course to upgrade her professional status which then led to further promotion and engagement in Continuing Professional Education]

A similar example was provided by a healthcare assistant, whose fear of exams had prevented her from talking any further qualifications.

"I became interested in Complementary Medicines, and I was having, oh gosh what do they call them, a chat with the ward manager who assesses what you've been doing over the last year, and she said 'Well, what are you going to do. Are you going to go through your whole life saying "No I can't?"'.... Go on, go for this'. And I said 'Yeah'. That was it."

Another nurse was preparing to discuss her need for some training in counselling at her next appraisal, in order to offer better support to patients at the oncology clinic where she worked. This was an example of a self-directed learner using the system, rather than an unconfident learner needing to be challenged and supported.

Given the project team approach, job descriptions were rarely significant in engineering. It was more a case of how best to use the assembled talent to get the job done. But in other sectors, the precise nature of the job was a frequent subject of discussion at appraisals, with modifications being used not only to reflect the changing demands but also for development purposes. Examples were cited of both job expansion and job redesign, the latter often occurring after an internal promotion rather than at an appraisal. In one case this involved expanding the work of a whole department by enlarging the roles of most of its members, with a consequent need for several staff to get further training for their new responsibilities:

"She's very good on helping people progress, she's very keen on post-grad studies. So quite a few of the radiographers here have been on the barium enema course because they're going to do barium enemas which takes some of the work load off the radiologists. Quite a few of us have been on the IV course so we can give (intravenous) injections ourselves, so we don't have to call the nurse or doctor to do it. Some of us have written up the instructions you know, as to what to give and how to give it and then we can get on and do it. So, she's very good from that point of view, but she can be a bit autocratic. She has a very forceful character." (Radiographer)

Not tea and sympathy but challenge, safety in numbers, and confidence that her staff were capable of doing what she asked of them.

A respondent from an engineering company described how he was being gradually eased into a team leadership role by his manager's phased withdrawal of support – an example of coaching, though not described as such.

"He's given me an area to work in, but he's also kept me sheltered from the ravages of the customer.... He's involved in the actual dates and time-scales when we've got to deliver the project; and I'm involved in getting to that point, in the day-to-day running of the team.... "

"Normally he's the guy whose chairing the meetings and I'm sitting in; but now he's there [only] 20% of the time, looking in and I'm chairing the weekly meetings and inviting him along. Not on this project, because it's such a short time-scale, but at some point down the line, I will be in charge of the whole project. I won't be the project manager, but I'll be the team leader in charge of delivering the software to the customer."

A nurse gave a somewhat similar but more opportunist example. She was involved as a witness in a disciplinary case, and rather nervous about it. Yet her manager realised that, if promoted, she would be expected to present such cases. So she involved her in discussions about the presentation, and debriefed her after the hearing, putting things into perspective.

"Soon I'm going to be there doing exactly the same thing and also eventually you've got to be able to present. I've got to get used to that sort of formality."

The manager as role model and/or expert

We encountered many examples in our research of people learning from watching how their managers handled people and situations or from tuning into their manager's expertise. This learning did not depend on whether their managers saw themselves as staff developers and appraised, mentored, action planned or coached. It depended on how their managers performed when they were present.

"I worked with a manager for a period of five years, who I believe to be one of the most capable people that I've ever met in the bank. I learnt an incredible amount from him just by watching him work. I don't think I would be doing the job I'm doing today unless I had that fabulous piece of experience of working with that one individual.... One thing I especially learned was to put the right people in the right job." (Senior Manager in a bank)

Negative models could be a source of learning as well as positive models, and often there were elements of both.

"I have learned an awful lot from him.... I still think some of the things he does are completely wrong ... my manager feels that to get things done, the way to do it is to shout at people ... I disagree with that method ... so that's one major disagreement that I've learned not to learn from [him] ... the number one thing he's always taught me ... [is] that you can never presume something, and you'll be okay. Always know something for definite." (PR Manager, public utility)

Many of the positive examples seemed to combine both personality and expertise.

"My immediate manager was a very dynamic person, a driving force ... I learned a lot of design for cost from him.... Also, the management of the qualification of the machine. It's one thing to build the machine but when you're doing a new machine you have to qualify at the end of it to prove that it does what it's supposed to do, and he was very good at quantifying how to do that and I learned a lot." (Development Engineer)

"He seemed to have a clarity of objective. If you were given a task by him it was very clearly specified.... He would produce examples to show how to present a document.... One also saw J in operation, not only in the local setting but also in the European [context].... There was modelling both on him as a person, and on examples of products [he showed you]." (Services Engineer)

Even from less sympathetic managers people learned about fairness, standards and loyalty to subordinates.

"The manager I worked for during that period was a very demanding person. He was one of those people who expect a lot of you but he made it clear exactly

what they expected. If you did something wrong he got you in and he told you off for doing it wrong. You did something right he praised you for doing right. And although he could be very critical of you inwardly, outwardly he would always give you total support. If he was dealing with someone else who was actually coming along and being critical about you he would support you to the Nth degree; but inwardly he might really be giving you a hard time." (Poduct Development Engineer)

The manager as creator of a climate which supports learning

Many of the most positive comments about managers related mainly to the effect they appeared to have on the climate in the workplace (Kozlowski and Hults, 1987; Tracey et al, 1995). Sometimes elements of the manager as staff developer or the manager as role model were also present, but this was just part of the story. What mattered most was that people felt it was a good working location where they were both stimulated and supported. It was especially interesting to note the wide range of personal styles which were described as being successful. The concepts underpinning people's praise for positive working environments, which were often contrasted with less positive examples, were achievement, support and participation.

The examples below demonstrate three contrasting styles of leadership, all praised for their high expectations, personal attention and development of individuals' confidence in their own capability.

"A wonderful manager, he was very good at making people feel they were important in their niche, and in encouraging them, giving that small amount of contact that is needed with a person to keep them going, which some managers do forget about. He actually comes round and says 'How are you, how are things going?' ... and he kept tabs on all the projects which I always thought was wonderful." (Engineer)

"I've noticed with D she'll never say 'That's not what I want', or 'Why haven't you got this back to me within an X amount of time?'. She's always so pleasant about it, not sort of excusing you or anything, but it's just the way she puts it, you know that she appreciates what's gone on, because she knows what's been happening or not,

why you haven't the report or whatever it is. She never gives the impression she's on your back. She has this really nice way of getting you to do it, regardless of the whole place being on fire, without making you feel dreadful about it. Because you know you've got to do it, but you've had 50 million other things going on, or you might have completely forgotten about it." (Nurse)

"He's innovative, he wants to drive things forward, he's quite a mixture; he's very autocratic in many ways, but he also expects a high level of independence in his staff. He'll say 'Just go ahead and do it'.... Yes I do feel incredibly supported and he does this, and if you go to him and say 'Look I don't quite understand why we're doing it this way, what about' he will listen and if he thinks it's reasonable he'll agree, so he's fairly open-minded." (Radiographer)

This last quotation provides an interesting mixture of challenge, participation and support. People need confidence in their manager as well as in their own capabilities.

"If your manager is in a bit of a flap, then it will just trickle down and you'll see the stress not only in the staff but eventually in the patients as well, and the doctors, and the domestic, and absolutely everybody. But because she's calm and efficient and makes it look so easy just not hard at all, then it just sort of spreads, and people are generally more confident; and they know that she's such a confident manager that everything just seems to go like clockwork." (Nurse)

This nurse also stressed the participative nature of management on her ward; as did a nursing assistant in another hospital.

"Quite frequently we would get together all the E grades, and A and J, and discuss some of the other issues that were going in the ward at the time. So I think that A's the type of manager who likes staff to be involved with decisions, so I think that we're always aware of things that are going on even if we're not directly involved in having to make those decisions.... Even though we're all part of a team, we each take on a certain amount of responsibility." (Nurse)

"If anything new is going to happen, then we get together. Sister will see as many of us as she can at one time, and talk to us about it and then a joint decision will be made. Or, if something is done above our heads then

we all have to discuss it afterwards, you know, and we try and alter it if it's not right. But we do get consulted, sister is very good at consulting us over the various changes that are going to happen. I wish the upper management were as good." (Nursing Assistant)

Another nurse appreciated a more low key, but still very supportive, approach:

"Initially, I don't think I appreciated how good a boss he was; he's not a good boss if you don't know what you're doing because he does tend to let you feel your way. He's not breathing over your shoulder. If I need him I go to him and if he wants to ask me to do something he'll come to me, otherwise he has his, I have mine, we get on. He's not trying to influence me, he advises me; so he'll never say 'You're going to do it this way', he'll say 'Have you thought about doing it that way?' He's very good at supporting you and pushing you forward as well, so you find other members of staff will come to you and say, 'Oh M's said that perhaps you could help us with this'. And sometimes you think 'For God's sake', but he's very good at trying to raise your profile so that you're noticed. I always get amazed round that place that, the bosses put their name on other people's work, I think it's terrible. And M will never do that, to the point that he'll insist that you put your name on the front of it and insist that you're there to discuss it, even if you don't want to present it to the board, he insists that you're sat there so you're seen to be the one with the knowledge." (Nurse)

Two engineers commented on environments which by most people's standards were good, but in their view could have been improved by giving greater attention to supporting new arrivals.

"In the engineering environment ... you could always go to people and they're always willing to help but you have to go and find the help, whereas when I moved into software everyone was coming up, offering advice, checking if I was OK.... Not only the supervisor, the whole team were very very good ... even now, you, you have to refer [to other people]. Because that guy really knows that particular area ... he can ... set you on a track to save you time."

"We have the most wonderful people here. They really want to help you, want to make sure you understand. But I think you don't get involved enough as a team, like with new people coming in there's this mentor thing. It's very much this new person comes in, you meet them and

slowly they might start getting socially involved with you, but on a work basis they're left on their own, to their own devices."

In neither case was this seen as a weakness in management, rather as a limitation in the peer group culture. This might reflect the dominance of 'projects' in product development companies and a corresponding lack of attention to line managers.

A concept frequently cited or implied by our respondents when describing factors influencing learning in their workplace was that of a 'blame-free culture'.

"If you take a film somebody will look at that, and 'cause it's so relaxed here, you don't take it personally that it's not as good as it could have been. Or, if you do a good film, they'll say 'Oh that's good, well done'. Because they quite happily will say when something's good, you don't mind when it's not so good." (Radiographer)

"He's an exceptional boss, I feel very safe to say 'I really screwed up here and I could have done better'." (Nurse)

People do not learn only from others' mistakes, as mentioned earlier, but also from their own. As one engineer commented:

"I don't really learn by being taught, I learn by cocking things up."

and another described how he learned forecasting:

"It was an acquired skill, basically I learned a lot and I made it up as I went along. You talk to people, you find out what they did, you copy it, you discuss with people what is working, what is not working; and what I basically did was to bring all the things I knew had gone wrong, and use that information to build a new system up in a different way, and make it work."

Conclusion

Our earlier paper 'Learning from other people at work' demonstrated the major contribution to performance of learning from other people within and beyond the workplace. This learning was either facilitated or constrained by (a) the organisation and allocation of work and (b) the social climate of the work environment. While our methodological approach led to a greater emphasis on positive evidence of learning, our respondents not only volunteered negative evidence but implicitly provided it when they compared their personal experiences of different work contexts. The clear implication, sometimes explicitly stated, was that important learning opportunities were missed in certain kinds of activity or situation, with negative consequences for the quality and speed of work. These claims about missed opportunities were based either on self-evident misses ("it would have saved a lot of time", "if only I had known..."') or on comparisons with other, more learning-friendly work environments. Thus they were credible assessments of what was feasible in those contexts, not untested aspirations driven by hypothetical models of a 'learning organisation'. Some respondents may have been more cognitively aware of, and positively disposed towards, recognising and using learning opportunities at work; but they still had to know whom to ask and to feel that their requests would be positively received. An important corollary would be an orientation towards offering help rather than waiting to be asked. The positive effect on confidence and performance of being consulted by colleagues should also be noted.

This paper argues that a major factor affecting a person's learning at work is the personality, interpersonal skills, knowledge and learning orientation of their manager. While approaches to management development normally emphasise motivation, productivity and appraisal, comparatively little attention is given to supporting the learning of subordinates, allocating and organising work, and creating a climate which promotes informal learning. This imbalance may result from ignorance about how much learning does (and how much more learning might) take place on the job. There are also implications for the selection of people for management roles. In most organisations the practical implications of strengthening informal learning for developing the individual and collective capabilities of employees are not yet understood.

The main implications for policy at national level lie in two areas: management training, as already discussed; and the limitations of the dominant mode of policy discourse. Problems are treated as well

defined and readily soluble, and therefore susceptible to formal, standardised types of training to clearly specified targets. Yet the concept of a knowledge-based economy and the metaphor of a learning organisation derive from recognition of the complexities and uncertainties of the modern world. Public discourse about training not only neglects informal learning but denies complexity by oversimplifying the processes and outcomes of learning and the factors that give rise to it.

References

Armstrong, M. and Baron, P. (1998) *Performance management: The new realities*, London: Institute for Personnel and Development

Bevan, S., Thompson, M. and Hirsch, W. (1992) *Performance management in the UK: An analysis of the issues*, London: Institute for Personnel and Development.

Bevan, S. and Hayday, S. (1994) *Toeing the line: Helping managers to manage people*, Research Report No 254, Brighton: Institute for Employment Studies.

Dubin, S.S. (1990) 'Maintaining competence through updating', in S.S. Dubin and S.L. Willis (eds) *Maintaining professional competence*, San Francisco, CA: Jossey-Bass.

Eraut, M., Alderton, J., Cole, G. and Senker, P. (1998a) *Development of knowledge and skills in employment*, Research Report No 5, Brighton: Institute of Education, University of Sussex.

Eraut, M., Alderton, J., Cole, G. and Senker, P. (1998b) 'Learning from other people at work', in F. Coffield (ed) *Learning at work*, Bristol: The Policy Press, pp 37-48.

Kozlowski, S.W.J. and Hults, B.M. (1987) 'An exploration of climates for technical updating and performance', *Personnel Psychology*, vol 40, pp 539-63.

McCauley, C.D., Ruderman, M.N., Ohlott, P.J. and Morrow, J.E. (1994) 'Assessing the developmental components of managerial jobs', *Journal of Applied Psychology*, vol 79, no 4, pp 544-60.

Tracey, J.B., Tannenbaum, S.I. and Kavanagh, M.J. (1995) 'Applying trained skills on the job: the importance of the work environment', *Journal of Applied Psychology*, vol 80, no 2, pp 239-52.

3

Young lives at risk in the 'futures' market: some policy concerns from ongoing research

Stephen J. Ball, Sheila Macrae and Meg Maguire

Introduction

This paper adumbrates a set of policy concerns identified in an ongoing research study of one small cohort of inner-city youth. The database of our study is narrow but deep, and represents certain specifics of the urban research setting. The policy concerns we discuss can be read as being limited by that narrowness and specificity but we would suggest from our review of other research that these are generic features of post-16 education and training; and the market setting we describe and the diversity of aspirations, opportunities and constraints we have found are typical of many other inner-city locations in the UK. Generally the claims we make for the worth of the research rest on complexity, depth and longitudinality rather than size or representativeness and this needs to be borne in mind when considering the policy concerns discussed below.

Our research attempts to capture and interpret the educational, work and domestic lives of young people as they engage with one education, training and labour market setting in South West London[1]. Our local market extends over an inner-city/ suburban setting based around the Northwark area of London (see Gewirtz et al, 1995) and is defined in terms of the expressed interests and choices of a cohort of Year 11 students from one comprehensive school – Northwark Park – and one Pupil Referral Unit (PRU). This local, lived market encompasses several different, small local education authorities that organise their schools' provision in different ways. The main players in this market are two 11-18 secondary schools, five Further Education (FE) colleges, a tertiary college, a denominational sixth form college and two Training and Enterprise Councils (TECs). Three other FE colleges, another sixth form college, and an 11-18 denominational school impinge upon the margins of this market – see Figure 1. We have engaged with the main groups of actors in this market: providers, that is, those offering education, training or employment; intermediaries, that is, those offering advice or support, including teachers, careers officers and parents; and consumers or choosers, that is, the young people themselves and their families.

Figure 1: Location of main providers of post-16 education and training

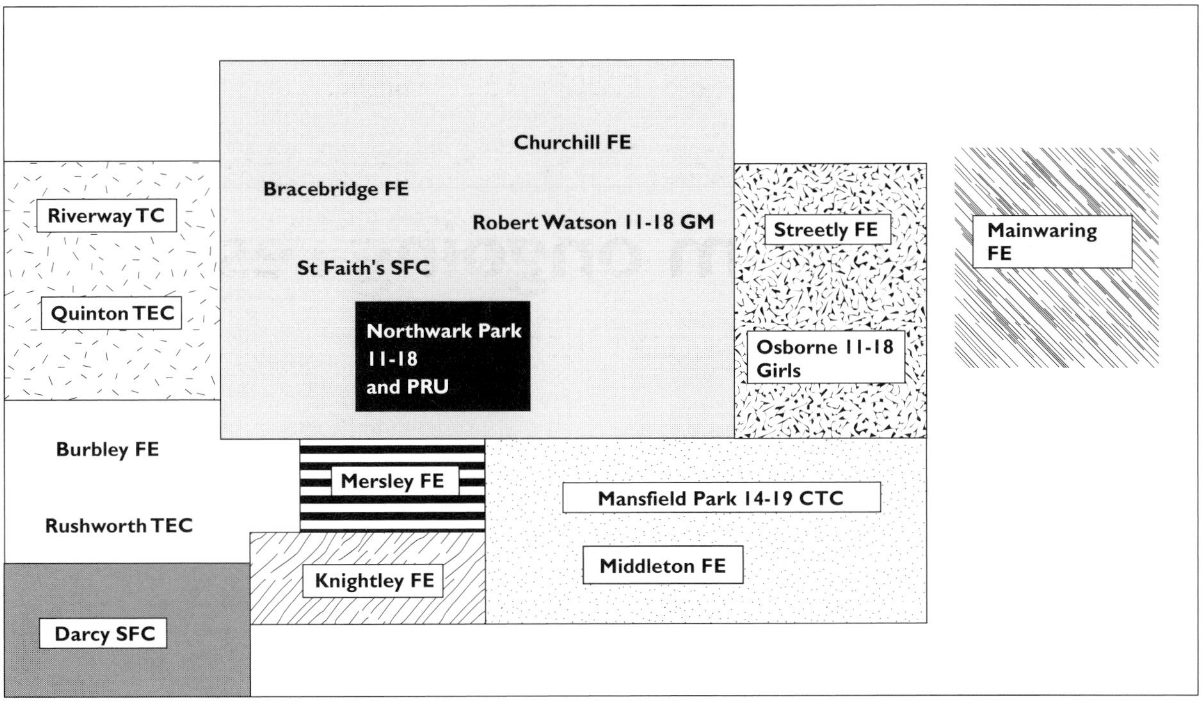

Note: shaded areas indicate nine different local education authorities

As indicated above, our data are based upon contacts initiated with a group of Year 11 students in 1995. Our original sample comprised a total of 110 students: 81 from the 11-18, mixed comprehensive school and 29 from the local PRU. From this cohort of students a smaller group was selected for in-depth study. This sub-sample was constituted to represent the range of Northwark Park students in terms of gender, social class, academic attainment, 'ethnicity' and destinations and routes from school to work and includes some young people who had already opted out of formal education. It consisted of 64 young people: 46 from the school and 18 from the PRU. They were interviewed once in each of the Spring and Summer terms of Year 11 and again at some point in their first year post-16. These young people were at the time of writing (September, 1998) in the second year of their post-16 experience and were being interviewed for the fourth time. We have also interviewed representatives of all major local providers, and collected and analysed some of their public documentation, and interviewed teachers, careers officers and a sample of parents.

Table 1: Youth markets students' routes (June 1997)

	Northwark Park	PRU	Total
A-level	12	0	12
GNVQ Advanced	1	0	0
GNVQ Intermediate	8	0	8
GNVQ Foundation	6	3	9
NVQ Level 1	2	4	6
NVQ Level 2	2	4	6
GCSE retakes	1	0	1
BTEC	1	0	1
Working	7	1	8
Army	0	1	1
Not working	4	4	8
Unknown	2	1	3
Total	**46**	**18**	**64**

Policy issues

The issues we have chosen to highlight here are diverse but some are closely interrelated. Most are explored in greater depth in other project papers. We have not attempted to ground them here in our data but have included a very small number of illustrative extracts. Some of the concerns are more obviously amenable to a direct policy response than others but we would argue that they all have immediate relevance to policy thinking about 'lifelong learning'.

Positioning in post-16 education and training

We begin with a very simple and very obvious but fundamental point. By the end of compulsory schooling, young people are positioned very differently in terms of their opportunities and interest in the post-16 education and training market (ETM). There are two main issues here.

First, despite the rhetoric of many of the policies and documents related to the ETM, significant numbers of young people emerge from school with very little choice or opportunity. Their school records and examination results and in some cases learning difficulties disqualify them from most routes on offer in the ETM. In what we have called 'the economy of student worth' such young people are of 'low' value. The post-16 ETM is not an open system. It is a complex, hierarchical and differentiated system. *And current policies work to exacerbate all of these features.* Choice as such is constrained in two ways. Obviously, some routes will be more or less available in relation to the academic profile of students at GCSE level. At the same time, although providers all aim to recruit above their target numbers (to increase the likelihood of achieving their Further Education Funding Council [FEFC] quotas), popular and 'successful' institutions will actually be in the position of doing the 'choosing' from among those who apply. "The orientations of schools, colleges and employers are still fundamentally selective rather than facilitative" (Banks et al, 1992, p 188). Institutions located in the post-16 market are increasingly driven by expediency: the need to recruit sufficient numbers of students in order to

maintain or maximise income, and in particular, the need to recruit 'good' students who will support the institution's reputation and market position. Institutions are also positioned differently in the market by virtue of their reputation and potential to select:

> *"I suppose we are lucky in that I can be a bit choosy. I mean, there are a number of people who don't even get so far as an interview. Either their report is not satisfactory. If they are from our partner schools yes, but I think, why should our staff who are really hassled, why should they take on other people's problems? I will just say that we are full, there are no places." (Vice-Principal, St Faith's Sixth Form College)*

Nonetheless, within the local market hierarchy some 'providers' have to manage and cope with the least desirable (and more costly) school leavers:

> *"We do tend to get the reputation of our provision being for low achievers and it is not, you know. We are fighting hard to say it is not. It is for young people for whom a work-based vocation is more appropriate. The fact that we do have to deal with young people who may have few skills, a low level of education and they may have social problems and an attitude problem. The fact that we also have to deal with them makes it difficult for us to attract a higher level client group." (Young People and Training Adviser, Rushworth TEC)*

Some sense of the 'economy of student worth' at work, which students are sought after and which are not, is conveyed in these comments, and one black young woman from our cohort who achieved three A-C grades at GCSE, offers a student's point of view:

> *"I think if I was an A-level type student then there would be pressure on me [to stay on], but because I am not, no one has said nothing to me about staying on. No one has encouraged me to stay or nothing. But I think because I am a C and D kind of person that is why, they really want the type of A-level people to stay and give the school a better reputation, so that is why I think no one has said nothing to me about staying because I wouldn't do nothing to improve the reputation."*

As noted above, GCSE coursework and examinations are the primary mechanism for and manifestation of the differential positioning of young people. Students either internalise the labels generated around GCSE performance or seek to define themselves in terms of alternative, resistant and sometimes destructive life-styles and selves. For many the 'realities' of GCSE performance finally destroy tentatively held aspirations. Through all this, what Bates and Riseborough (1993, p 9) call the "deep sub-structures of inequality" re-emerge clearly, the differentiation of routes and 'spaces' of opportunity are reproductive of social class divisions – "privilege and disadvantage are ploughed into youth careers through family and education but most importantly at the interface between the two spheres" (p 9). (A point we shall return to later.) What Bates and Riseborough describe as the "vastness of the gulf between the opportunities of young people" (p 11) seems undiminished by the new regimes of schooling and training (cf the recent reports from Dearing [1996], Kennedy [1997] and NIACE [1996].

Second, and it is here that the first challenge in producing what the Fryer Report calls "a revolution in attitudes" lies (Fryer, 1997), for some students the end of compulsory schooling is very much, at least for the time being, a definite end point to their appetite for education. Post-16 choices for such young people are heavily constrained by economic circumstances – the non-existent youth labour market in our locality – and inhibited by 'learner identities' (Rees et al, 1997) which may be at best estranged, or at worst 'damaged'; although "learning identities are not simply the product of formal education" (p 493). Leaving school may be the only immediate goal in play for many students, although for some there may be the possibility of a fresh start of some kind. As Bynner et al (1997) found, "those young people who had left the education system at the earliest possible age were becoming increasingly disadvantaged later on" (p 126).

"Most people, you know, they have been in school for so many years they just want to get on with their lives now. They've had enough of sitting in classrooms, they're bored, they just want to get a job and some money ... they want a fresh start, a job, a new life, not more writing and learning things that nobody cares about."

Indeed, by the time of the examinations a significant number has already 'chosen otherwise' and leave or are excluded from school before completing their GCSE courses. The pressures of the secondary school market place and local league table competition would appear to be increasing the number of school-age youngsters 'out-of-school' (Gewirtz et al, 1995).

Policy issues

The important point here for researchers and policy makers is that to focus attention on the post-16 ETM and lifelong learning as objects of concern is to miss the point. A proper understanding of patterns of participation in post-16 education and training must rest upon analysis of the positionings, educational aspirations and learning identities produced by the compulsory sector. Our compulsory system as presently organised is not geared to inclusivity or achieving maximum post-16 participation. Indeed many of the policies currently in play work directly against this goal. A policy for lifelong learning needs to begin at the age of three not 16.

Market dysfunctions

Overall, the market setting in which our research is located can be characterised in a variety of ways. It might well be thought of, as one respondent described it, a "cut throat" market (Deputy Head of Faculty, FE College), or put another way, from the point of view of the providers: "it's grow or die" (Student Counsellor, FE College). This 'cut throat' quality, which is generated in part by the proximity of multiple providers, in part by the entry of new players, and in good measure by the rigours of the FE funding regime itself, is evidenced in a variety of ways in the market behaviour of, and relationships between, providers. Markets reward shrewdness rather than principle and privilege the values of competition over 'professional' values (Gewirtz et al, 1993; Ball et al, 1994). In other words, education markets, like other markets, are driven by self-interest. As one respondent put it: "the College cannot afford to take a moral stance". On the one side is the self-interest of consumers who 'choose' in terms of their individual interests (in all senses of the word) and on the other that of producers aiming to thrive, or at least survive (Gewirtz et al, 1995). The 'cut throat' quality and values of competition increasingly in play in this market encourage and make possible a particular variety of actions and tactics. Various respondents identified new forms of inter-institutional behaviour emerging in the context of market relations: new rivalries and competition, the use of mis-information, marketing madness and impression management, and 'ethical drift'. Our analysis of data suggests that it is certainly questionable whether these new forms of behaviour best serve the needs and interests of all students or are effectively related to the needs of the economy or local communities or make best use of scarce resources. The application of Bartlett and Le Grand's (1993) criteria for the evaluation of quasi-market reforms – efficiency, responsiveness, choice and equity – will serve to summarise our findings.

As far as productive efficiency is concerned, the picture is patchy. Indirect evidence would suggest that the duplication of courses may increase costs-per-unit in some institutions while reducing quality – at least in the short term. Against this the requirements of expansion are increasing the intensity of plant use but the market itself involves new costs in marketing, environmental improvements, provision of support services and so on. Where expansion targets are met these costs may be offset against new income, although as elsewhere the majority of providers in this local market have not met their income targets. The creation of new sixth forms and the maintenance of small sixth forms are also dubious on cost and quality grounds. Some schools heavily subsidise their sixth form provision from their 11-16 income in order to attract clients at age 11.

On the face of it, responsiveness has improved. The FEFC funding regime certainly encourages providers to attend carefully to their potential markets and to expand their range of courses even where the number of students completing some courses far outnumber job vacancies in the field. The funding regime has also encouraged the development of pastoral and counselling systems aimed at better support for and retention of students, although drop-out from courses still seems to run at a relatively high level (and Department for Education and Employment figures on age participation do not seem to take this into account). Clearly, some of the new client-centredness of post-16 providers is cosmetic. Alongside this there is also

a much greater incentive towards what might be called 'over-responsiveness'. That is: (a) running courses for which the provider has little expertise and for which there are few occupational opportunities; (b) admitting students to courses for which they are ill-suited; (c) giving misleading information and advice to students (see also Schagen et al, 1996); and (d) moving entry requirements in response to changes in demand. The disciplines of the market set professional ethics over and against the ethics of the marketplace (Ball, 1998). The appearance of greater responsiveness (market driven) does not ensure that students' needs are always met appropriately (professional judgement).

A contiguous post-16 market, as in the case here, clearly offers, at least in general terms, choice and diversity to consumers and choice is a powerful animating and change mechanism in this setting. All of the institutions in this market are highly competitively aware. They are all self-conscious of their public image and reputation. Those that are able to, spend considerable sums on marketing and promotion. There is a dual process at work in all this; on the one hand, specialist provision is breaking down as institutions seek new clients; on the other, there are new kinds of niches being exploited or explored. However, the role of market information as a basis for effective choice making is problematic. Information flows are erratic and inefficient. The access of students to formal information is often limited by intermediaries who have vested interests. Furthermore, as noted already, choice is not equally available to all. Some providers still exercise considerable power in the market place by selecting their entry as a means of maintaining performance or exclusivity or keeping down costs.

Thus, on the one hand, the behaviour of institutions within our ETM appears to generate a number of significant inefficiencies and duplications, it produces dis-coordination, it encourages segmentation, differentiation and exclusion, it inhibits information flow, it encourages short-termism, and it throws up ethical dilemmas, the resolution of which sometimes work against student interests. The market is not simply a new mechanism of service provision; it is a new culture and values system. It also 'calls up' and valorises class, gender and racial categories which work systematically against the interests of some students. On the other hand, there are positive outcomes from this market 'behaviour' – for example, the development of systems to improve retention, a greater attention to some 'minority' interests and greater awareness of students with special educational needs, and greater flexibility in the modes of delivery of courses.

Policy issues

The market form seems singularly ill-equipped to deliver a system of education and training focused upon the needs of all learners, that is understandable and transparent, and which makes the most effective use of available resources. For certain, the market form does nothing to achieve the sort of 'simplification and integration' (argued for by Fryer, 1997, p 6) and, by definition, it works to eradicate "partnerships[2], planning and collaboration" (p 7); our market is marked by insecurity, high anxiety, ruthlessness, suspicion, duplication, 'knocking copy' and poaching.

Race and the market

The post-16 ETM is suffused, structured and inflected by 'race' and racism. 'Race' is a significant analytical category in relation to all of the issues with which we are concerned[3]: student choice, provider recruitment and marketing, access to courses and retention. In terms of Gillborn's (1995) analysis of policy discourses and 'race', the distribution and deployment of racial categories in this market is complex but nonetheless patterned. "People routinely adopt 'race' thinking" (Gillborn, 1995, p 5). 'Race' is a prime consideration in the representations 'given' and 'given off' (Goffman, 1971) by provider institutions in their marketing and recruitment activities. Here the recruitment of minority ethnic students is constructed by some providers as a 'problem' and by others as an 'opportunity'. 'Race' also informs the choices made by both black and white parents and students.

The colleges (FE, sixth form and tertiary) in our local market have distinct, widely shared racial identities based on a combination of location and patterns of attendance. They are part of a complex social and racial geography which reflects what Keith and Cross (1993, p 26) refer to as "the city as, in part, a nested series of overlapping locales through which the different processes and scales of racialisation are realised". The location and identities of the colleges interact with racialised choosing to produce a south-westerly movement of students, both black and white, away from the inner-city schools and colleges into the suburbs (cf OECD, 1994). In some of the suburban FE colleges this produces a marked mismatch between the student population and the local residential population. (Northwark is approximately 80% white, whereas Bracebridge College in Northwark has approximately 80% minority ethnic students; Mersley has a minority ethnic population of 16%, whereas Mersley College has 50% minority ethnic students, etc.) This drift has knock-on effects for the reputation of the receiving colleges which drives 'local' choices further south and west. Within this racialised market colleges interpret and accommodate 'race' issues in different ways. Those colleges located in areas with high proportions of minority ethnic families or which attract large numbers of minority ethnic students appear to be attempting to maximise their recruitment by adopting strategies which they see as likely to encourage and support the participation of these students (see Ball et al, 1998, for further discussion). In those colleges occupying market positions and locations in predominantly white areas the racialisation of their market behaviour is also different. For those colleges which see white middle-class students interested in A-level courses as their main target audience, minority ethnic and particularly African-Caribbean male students can be seen as a 'problem'. Again this is part of the 'economy of student worth' within the ETM. Their presence and visibility is often regarded more directly as a 'liability' in terms of their impact on the reputation or perception of their college among white choosers. This is the case, for example, at Burbley where the marketing manager finds himself caught between the college's commitment to a policy of equal opportunities and the feelings of some staff that the behaviour of black students is a deterrent to highly valued, white, A-level students.

"The problem is that teachers tend to, you know, you see a lot of black youngsters they do over react, that is true. Well, the view has been put that we, to give you an

example of that, we do insist on a no smoking policy in the college so it means at certain times of the day the steps just behind you there are absolutely packed with students obviously puffing away, you see, and most of them tend to be black and to be girls as well, you know, both white and black and black males, and it has been said to me once or twice that we should try and get rid of that really, and people have quoted parents saying that they find it quite off-putting if they come to the college for the first time to push their way through that kind of mob, you know. A lot of the white middle-class parents don't care for all these black students and, you know, you have to be careful not to alienate them because they are our bread and butter, you know, but you can't be seen to agree with them either. I don't think the black youngsters are in themselves violent but it is just that people perceive them to be violent, you know.... West Indians tend to be quite out-going I think is the word and if you are not used to that, it can be off-putting. Yes it is a slight problem. People here compare us with Darcy College. I don't know if that is one of the colleges you are looking at. It is a sixth form college and of course they do A-levels in a nice white middle-class group and hence a lot of teachers, obviously teaching A-levels, would like us to get that sort of set up here, you know. But I think in the main we accept the whole equal opportunities thing and, as I say, if you look at the prospectus I hope you find the right balance, you know." (Marketing Manager, Burbley FE College)

There is a telling slippage in this extract from a 'problem' of smoking to the possibility of violence. Underlying these comments and others in our data is what Miles (1989) calls the "practical adequacy of racism" in the sense that they refract "in thought certain observed regularities, and construct(s) a casual interpretation which can be presented as consistent with those regularities and which serves as a solution to perceived problems" (p 80). And as Gillborn (1995) has noted in his work on comprehensive schools, there is a displacement of blame onto white parents. Similar concerns and sentiments were expressed by staff responsible for recruitment at Riverway Tertiary College. Riverway itself is predominantly white, 5.5% of the population are minority ethnic, Irish being the largest single group. However, the college attracts students from well beyond the boundaries of Riverway and is a recipient of large numbers of the 'flight' choices noted earlier. In terms of income this inflow is a clear benefit. However, this again

creates some disquiet among staff when the demography of the college is commented upon by prospective parents from Riverway (see also Bagley, 1996, p 574).

It could be said, however, that we are unable to demonstrate conclusively that these mechanisms and perspectives are specific to a market system or did not exist before. We are certainly not suggesting that the pre-market post-16 regime was devoid of institutional racism. However, we think there is enough evidence in the specifics of the initiatives, responses and orientations in our data to indicate a variety of ways in which the FE market, and what we have called elsewhere its 'debased ethics' (Ball et al, 1998), forged in response to the draconian FEFC funding regime, 'valorise' and objectify students in racial terms.

There is another level to this issue in as much that the FE as opposed to the post-16 school sector 'over-recruits' minority ethnic students (Cheng, 1995), although overall higher proportions of black and Asian students also stay on post-16 compared with white students. The FE sector is regarded as a 'second chance' by many minority ethnic students who have had 'unsatisfactory' experiences in the school sector.

The processes described here cut across the arguments presented by market advocates, that because they have no intentionality markets cannot by definition be racist. What we see in the operation of the market, it would be argued by such advocates, is 'simply' the importation of 'race thinking' embedded in the wider society. To a degree this is true. The market is not the progenitor of racism. But we are suggesting that the market 'calls up', to an extent legitimates, and valorises 'race' as a category in choice making, in the competition between institutions and in the way that institutions present and market themselves. Thus, the market is a particular manifestation of one form of 'institutional racism', that is: "circumstances where exclusionary practices arise from, and therefore embody a racist discourse but which may no longer be explicitly justified by such a discourse" (Miles, 1989, p 84)[4]. Furthermore, the insertion and development of the market form has also played a part generally in the marginalisation or elimination of 'anti-racist' policies and debates about 'race' at the local and institutional level, however limited the impact of these may have been on the extent of racism and racial discrimination (Solomos, 1993). Nonetheless, we have also noted some ways in which, in particular settings, market perspectives have some kinds of positive, if rather weak, effects (Ball et al, 1997).

The inter-play of 'race' and space is also important in making sense of the organisation of our local market; spatial practices "are never neutral in social affairs. They always express some kind of class or other social content, and are more often than not the focus of intense social struggle" (Harvey, 1989, p 239). As noted above, the schools and colleges are constrained, in different ways, by material spatial practices, and each operates within an idiosyncratic spatial 'discourse'. This is both a matter of local geography, transport, physical access and local demography and the 'communities' that colleges 'serve', as well as the production of reputations based on location. In simple terms, within the ETM colleges are labelled and constrained by where they are and which students they currently recruit.

Turning to the 'choices' of young people, it is important to be clear that 'race' is not always the predominant category in the students' choices of post-16 education and training. It is embedded in, and interrelates in, complex ways with a range of other concerns, worries, priorities and interests. 'Race' is part of the students' complex topography of choice. It is embedded for most, but not all, in their personal social geographies, social stereotypes and general fearfulness about the future. "I don't know. I haven't experienced any prejudice against me or anything but it could be out there in the big wide world. I don't know yet" (Chinese student). Occasionally it does come to the forefront. However, very often it is a subordinate issue, particularly when special vocational interests or material constraints or lack of opportunity or alternatives are prominent. 'Race' also means different things to different students in their landscape of choice.

For both black and white students their spatial practices within the education market are imbued with racial meanings (and indeed class meanings). While such practices "abound in subtleties and complexities" they are "closely implicated in

processes of reproduction and transformation of social relations" (Harvey, 1989, p 218). The education market in this locality provides the possibility of 'escape' for some (the 'flight' referred to earlier), while leaving untouched, and indeed reinforcing, the racialised categorisation of space and spatial separation, and it erects barriers for others. To illustrate, most of our students would not consider or were extremely wary of what they regarded as 'black colleges'. Here, an African-Caribbean young woman, is talking about Bracebridge College.

D: "I have been there before. I don't like it. It is too shabby."

S: "What do you mean? Tell me about it being shabby."

D: "It is all rough people go to that college. I want to go to a nice, smart college where I can just learn, without getting hassled or talked to. I just want to go there, do my work, go home and relax. It's all rough, shabby people who don't want to do no work. They just go there and hang around. I've done enough of that. I need to learn and I want to go to a smart college where I don't know nobody so nobody can drag me in, give me hassle and stop me learning because if I went there I might just be like them and not go to lessons and that. There is too many shabby black boys go to that one anyway."

The market is an arena of struggle for social advantage but it depoliticises 'race' (and class) issues, subsuming them within the language of marketing, recruitment and the individualisation of choice. Racism is reworked into the abstract 'disciplines' of market forces and the disaggregated dynamics of consumer choice. Social justice is marginalised and neutralised as a concern in the privatised mechanics of choice and the technical rigours of marketing. Survivalism is constantly asserted over principle or values.

Having chosen to highlight issues of 'race', which do have a particular salience in the FE sector, we would also want to acknowledge the inter-relationships of social class and special needs in the pattern of inequalities generated by the ETM, and the increasing complexity and instability of youth identities in the city. Within the 'economy of student worth' these race, class and special needs are compounded in the construction of patterns of advantage and disadvantage.

Policy issues

There are several complex issues involved here and again we would highlight the importance of seeing the pattern of opportunities in the post-16 ETM in relation to the outcomes and effects of compulsory schooling. We would also want to underline the significance of the value changes which arise from the workings of the ETM. The values of the market and the pressures of survival are frequently incompatible with equal opportunity policies. And in more general terms the racialisation of the ETM may be storing up problems for future race relations in the UK.

Making choices

One of the particular strengths of in-depth, qualitative research is the possibility it offers of insight into the individual meanings and interpretations which underlie actions and decision making. If, as Fryer (1997, p 29) suggests, "The focus of policy and practice [for lifelong learning] should be learners themselves ...", we need to know a great deal more about the attitudes, motivations and inhibitions which young people bring to the ETM.

Imagined futures

For many of our young people their initial post-16 choices are based upon weak commitments, fuzziness about the future and limited information. Some appear to take pre-emptive decisions about courses, institutions and possible careers which in virtually every case turn into 'false starts'. For these, personal uncertainties and lack of information were in the ascendant over a coherent sense of an effective decision-making self – the experiences, resources and motivations relevant for such a construction were unevenly distributed across the sample. But it is important to see this fuzziness and the false starts as in part at least a response to a social context of uncertainties. Formal careers advice seems to be of little importance, or apparent use to most students, whereas the advice and experiences

of friends and relatives are crucial[5]. And none of the thinking ahead that is expected of students in Year 11 is helped by the considerable pressures of GCSE coursework completion and examination revision[6]. Many students, in retrospect, talked about leaving their post-16 decision 'too late'. Unresearched, unstable or desperate choices were sometimes turned into firm decisions about routes and courses by the pressure of time, chance interventions or the influence of significant others. Hodkinson et al (1996) make a similar point:

> *The lack of knowledge and confidence and relative powerlessness of many young people, together with the pragmatically rational ways in which they made career decisions, meant that many did not shop around for placements or training. The use of local networks to find placements often combined with such decision-making to restrict 'choice' to simply saying yes or no to a particular opportunity. (Hodkinson et al, 1996, p 124)*

Various familial resources are important here: the 'educational inheritance' of parents in particular (Edwards et al, 1989). One way of making sense of the differences in decision making at this point is in relation to the role of 'imagined futures' in the motivations and hopes of young people. Crudely, three groups of young people are identifiable. For some their 'imagined futures' are relatively clear, relatively stable and relatively possible. This group consists almost entirely of those on an A-level/HE route and those with a long-standing personal interest commitment – horses, the RAF, acting, dancing, and so on.

For a second group their 'imagined futures' are vague, relatively unstable and beset with uncertainties. This group is made up of two sets of young people. The first set are A-level and GNVQ students who feel the need for more qualifications but have vague and often very general 'career' interests – computers, business, design, 'running my own business'. The second set are those whose interest is solely in 'getting work'. They want a job, a car, a flat and a summer holiday and maybe a girlfriend or boyfriend. The type of job does not matter as long as it is a 'proper job' – that is, not part of a training scheme, not agency work. The futures here are short term. The routes and futures which had been available to such young people in previous generations have been swept away by the changes in the local economy and labour market, but they remain powerfully present in the hopes and imaginations of some young people.

The third group are unable to articulate an 'imagined future' which can provide a focus for decision making. They may display what looks like a sense of aimlessness, or see their life in terms of the necessities of 'getting by', 'making out' and coping, on a day-to-day basis, or are overtaken or dominated by domestic events 'beyond their control'; for example, pregnancy, poverty, homelessness, family breakdown, personal crises. In each case an ideal-type 'learner identity' and attendant "view of the process of learning" (Rees et al, 1997, p 493) may be discerned, and so "alternative courses of educational action are evaluated" (p 493) accordingly.

Attitudes and cultures of learning

We have already said something about those young people who, based on their experience to date of 'learning', display no further interest in education. Indeed, many have developed a marked aversion to further 'learning'. Here we want to re-visit, briefly, those young people who do at least begin post-16 education or training courses. At the risk of confusion we will again present them through a four-fold typology – hangers-in, notional acceptors, pragmatic acceptors and embedded. Here we see, for some, the reinvestment and development of existing, constructive 'learner identities', and for others, attempts to reconstruct or manage damaged identities.

Hangers-in

In this category is a mixture of young people, but they are generally 'low achievers' who, ideally, would like to find a job. Many are easily influenced by teachers, careers advisers and friends and several stayed on at Northwark Park for the school's sixth form. Others have 'done a geographical', that is, wanting to escape an unfavourable learning environment, believing that the 'grass would be greener' in another institution. For a number of these young people, many of the difficulties that had troubled them at school were being re-enacted in their new places of education and training. This has been particularly true of PRU students, several of

whom began the post-16 academic year with high hopes of a fresh start. The vast majority of these 'hangers-in', so called because of their tenuous hold on FE, are on NVQ Level 1 or 2 or GNVQ Foundation courses and many of their concerns and complaints focus on other students in their classes whom they describe as disruptive and who make unreasonable demands on over-worked teaching staff. Many of the hangers-in had made their college arrangements rather late and several spoke of being glad to have been accepted on courses. None had done particularly well in their GCSEs and some had to overcome social and emotional difficulties in order to find placements. None appeared to have made friends in their new institutions and several found that loneliness compounded their problems. They are, perhaps, as Ainley and Green (1996, p 23) put it, "going nowhere very quickly".

Notional acceptors

In this category we have those young people who notionally accept the need for FE and training but who behave as if education happens by a process of osmosis: by simply being present in the school or college it is somehow possible to 'become educated' even when playing cards in the common room. Many would probably be happier in work or on Network Training but pay lip-service to further academic study, somehow seeing it as 'better' and more likely to lead to a 'good job' than any other route. Some such acceptors may drop out or change programmes fairly quickly. Others will settle down when they realise that effort is needed on their part.

Pragmatic acceptors

As stated above, almost all students saw the necessity for study beyond the age of 16 but they varied considerably in their perceptions of the amount, depth and length of study needed to increase their chances of a 'good job'. These pragmatic acceptors are prepared to undertake, on average, two further years of study, after which they will be looking for employment. Their sole aim is to improve their employment prospects. "No I'm not looking for a job now, not yet [end of Year 11]. You've got to be trained. I'm going to college; I'm going to do catering and then I'll be looking for a job.... I'll be 18 by then; you can get jobs when you're 18." (PRU student). It may well be that the majority of learners in this country fall into the pragmatic acceptors category.

Such students appear not to engage fully with the learning process but are driven by the desire for further credentialisation. Educational experiences are rarely if ever portrayed as an end in themselves, as intrinsically worthwhile, or as potentially involving or stimulating. Rather, education is presented as a cumulative necessity, something that must be 'done' and 'got' as a means to other ends – getting a job. This orientation is ramified by modes of assessment which reduce the curriculum to atomised competencies and breaks learning down into stages and levels to be 'got through'.

Embedded

In this category are 'active-choosers' (see Macrae et al, 1996) from mainly middle-class homes and almost all are following A-level courses. These students had prepared well for the post-16 transition, considering a wide range of options and visiting a number of colleges before making their choice. All the young people who fitted best into this category had left Northwark Park for colleges with good academic reputations and were mostly very satisfied with their choice of institution and A-level course. The majority of these students have fairly well worked-through career aspirations and the majority intend to go on to university after college. The embedded students spoke with enthusiasm about the new friends they had made and the learning opportunities that had opened up for them. For these young people post-16 education is an extension and development of their previous educational experiences: a sense of achievement, self-esteem and worthwhileness predominates in their accounts. Their current learning and college work are located meaningfully, for them, in a long-term life plan and a personal narrative. They are 'becoming somebody' in the sense of being able to fulfil ambitions and relate their current life and work to an anticipated future.

In contrast, the acceptors (both the notional and pragmatic), are typically unable to locate their current educational experiences in the same meaningful way; their commitments to learning are interwoven with uncertainty, a lack of positive direction and often a lack of positive reinforcement or self-worth in relation to their education and work. These young people are caught within the ideology and the rhetorics of the learning society and the material deprivations and lack of opportunity of the inner-city labour market; hoping rather than aspiring and faced with a mismatch between their desires, interests and values and what they experience as the sterile and alienating vocationalism of the ETM.

Policy issues

For many young people the rhetorics of the learning society and getting qualifications and acquiring skills are not connected either to meaningful learning experiences or to the realities of their local, lived, labour market. Self-worth, personal satisfaction, identity and personal development seem to have no place in the education and training agenda of the competitive state. Many of those who experience the offerings of the ETM are simply frustrated and impatient. Education and training come to be seen as personally irrelevant or as simply holding locations, somewhere to be in the hope that something better will come along. Again it is important to look back at compulsory schooling and the range of 'learner identities' being produced. An overall strategy of lifelong learning must address this. The value of and effects of the GCSE examination system also need serious reassessment. Is such a system at 16 any longer relevant? It must be considered a major barrier to the achievement of an inclusive education system based on the firm expectation of all students continuing in education and training until at least the age of 18. In particular the GCSEs and the local league tables which are based upon them are oriented to the needs of high achieving students to the abject neglect of low achievers.

Careers advice and grapevine knowledge

From our interviews with students and with the formal intermediaries it was evident there was a significant mismatch between the rhetoric of careers advice and the practice as experienced by the 'client group.' In our locale, the Careers Service underwent a process of privatisation as our project started. The service contract requires that the careers officers ensure that all school leavers are interviewed and action plans are completed. These become the 'evidence' of task completion and contract compliance in the privatised service. However, the vast majority of the students reported unease and dissatisfaction with the support they received from the service and their school. The majority of students reported that the interviews were of little or no use and very few found the advice or information provided to be relevant to their needs. The timing of the interviews was also a problem. Most students were preoccupied with GCSE coursework completion and examination revision. But some students found that the interviews acted as a catalyst and served to remind them of the need to think seriously about post-16 possibilities, and a few spoke positively about the advice or information they received. The following extracts best convey a sense of the students' evaluation of the Careers Service:

K: "Basically the woman came in and just asked what would we like to do, but I didn't really have an idea exactly what I wanted to do, and she said because of my grades would I like to do an A-level or whatever. She did explain it but not so I can understand it that good."

L: "It was okay but I sort of ... when I, like, said I wanted to do computers and design and things and they went off a bit too far because they were handing out leaflets about Art College and that. I am not really sure what to say about that.... I just got a bit sort of confused really."

C: "We had a careers interview but I don't think that helped me at all, because I still have no idea what I am going to do and we have careers once a week. That is sort of, like, we do a little project on drugs or leaving home and recently we have done things, like, we could after school and now we are writing our Record of Achievement, but not really much careers advice."

M: "Has anybody given you anything to read?"

C: "No."

M: "Nobody has given you any information?"

C: "Well sort of, like little bits of information, nothing that is really helpful. Anything like that."

As noted, for a few students their careers interview did have a galvanising effect.

S: "It was very useful. It made me actually get up and go because I was dithering a bit. I wasn't sure where I wanted to head. I knew what I wanted to do, that I wanted to do performing arts but with the exams and everything you think of going to college as the last thing. They just told me what was optional and that and told me places to go. She gave me a few brochures of places that I could go and phone numbers and gave me her opinions on what would best suit me. So that was quite helpful."

As far as their own teachers were concerned many students were aware that competition for recruitment post-16 meant that the school staff were reluctant to suggest other destinations. In-house advice was thoroughly compromised by the market – a recent National Federation for Educational Research (NFER) survey has made the same point (Schagen et al, 1996).

Almost without exception other formal and 'official' sources of information are regarded with some suspicion – especially college brochures – or simply as 'uninformative'. We have described this as 'cold knowledge', it usually does not tell the young people what they want to know and it lacks credibility (Ball and Vincent, 1998). What is valued is 'hot knowledge'; that is, first or second hand, experiential and personal. 'Hot knowledge' is usually evaluative and unequivocal. Such 'hot knowledge' is often absolutely decisive in making a choice or rejecting an institution entirely. It is also particularly valued because the evaluations, advice, comment are often tailored to the personal characteristics of the individual. For some students, friends are as, or even more, important than parents in constructing possible futures. Friendships are arenas in which possibilities can be explored and tested, and are a source of first-hand experience of routes and opportunities inside education and training or beyond.

Policy issues

Our research raises serious questions about the effectiveness of careers advice in the current ETM context. The National Curriculum requirements have reduced the time devoted to careers work and the pressures of retention in 11-18 schools encourage 'protectionism'. We would reiterate the point made in the Fryer Report about the "inadequate or insufficiently available impartial guidance and counselling for would-be learners" (1997, p 21). We would also want to draw attention to the distinction between information and publicity. Provider publications have moved decisively from the former to the latter. The whole system of careers advice and the effects of privatisation on the work of the Careers Service seem in urgent need of investigation and review.

Families and choice

In almost all families parents provide a general framework of aspirations and hopes for their children, a space within which choices are made and validated[7]. Most parents were described in this way in our data (Macrae, 1997). From our reading of existing research we were surprised by the level of involvement of parents in the 'choices' made by young people. Families typically acted as what Foskett and Hesketh (1996) call 'composite consumers', although mothers frequently played the key role and were most often involved in 'hands on' choice work (phoning, collecting materials, arranging visits). However, in some cases 'support' is more abstract than real. Some parents have clear aspirations for their children and are proactive and interventionary in choice making. Others cede decision making to their child while expressing concerns or giving their backing to the choices explored by their sons and daughters. The young people operate within a "framed field of reference" (Foskett and Hesketh, 1996) established by their parents. For those parents who have no personal experience of further education purposeful intervention is sometimes difficult. These differences tend to polarise on social class lines with exceptions like aspiring migrant or refugee parents (see West and Varlaam, 1991; Thomas and Dennison, 1991; Reay and Ball 1997).

Families and friendships also differ in their access to emotional capital (Reay, 1996), that is, in their ability to mobilise and deploy emotional involvement and support. Reay argues in particular that social class and economic factors affect mothers' ability to

"divert their emotional involvement into generating academic profits for their children" (p 4).

There were also residual traces of more practical functions of the family in providing access to jobs or job opportunities – a number of the students talked about the importance of local employment contacts. Such contacts and local social and work relations certainly remained important in setting up work experience placements or getting part-time jobs. But the recent changes in the local economic/industrial structure meant that some families had been deskilled and had little 'really useful knowledge' to offer their children.

Indeed almost all of the parents we interviewed, from whatever social background, expressed uncertainty about, and ignorance of, the range of institutions, routes and qualifications on offer. Even those families who had already had one child go through the post-16 transition indicated continuing confusion. But as we have tried to indicate some families have more cultural and emotional resources and financial capacity to support and facilitate their children's 'choices' than do others. For a few of our young people choice of educational route or location, or choice between work and education was simply a matter of money. They or their families needed a wage coming in and could not afford the opportunity costs of education and training. Ironically once in work the New Deal training scheme (which is only for the unemployed) was ruled out for these young people (see also Herbert and Callender, 1998).

Policy issues

Again our research underlines the need for a more transparent and simpler structure for post-16 provision. The inherent complexity and the frequent changes in the qualifications, institutions, routes, financing and so on is compounded by the competition between, and market behaviours of, providers. Dislocation and incoherence are the result, even for those within the system. Our work also indicates how the market/consumer system tends to reinforce disadvantage for those families without the relevant resources or appropriate educational inheritance to discriminate effectively and operate proactively in the deregulated ETM.

Consumer skills and values are unevenly distributed across the population. Most market policies take choosers to be the same. Such policies are decontextualised, ignoring well-established class, race and gender differences, and trade upon the social practices and values of the middle class.

Conclusion

All too often it seems that the sectoral, disciplinary and research specialisation divisions which separate school-based research from FE and training/labour market research feed into and replicate a policy disposition. This frequently views compulsory schooling and post-16 education and training as distinct social and political 'problems'. And yet 'choices' made at 16 are decisively shaped, marked and 'positioned' by young people's experiences of success and 'failure' at school. To a large extent the 'problems' of poor participation, fragile motivation and status differentiation in post-16 education and training are rooted in compulsory schooling. Roberts (1993) commenting on data from the ESRC 16-19 initiative notes: "Indeed, qualifications earned by age 16 proved the best single predictor of the directions that individuals' careers would then take, particularly whether they would remain in full-time education and, if so, on which courses" (Roberts, 1993, p 230). Little seems to have changed. Indeed, selection, competition, congestion in the turbulent field of post-16 ETM articulate with, ramify and inflect the differentiating effects of the compulsory phase. The post-16 ETM 'valorises' certain resources which are unevenly distributed across the population. The pressures of competition also, at least in the kind of market we are researching, often set the interests of providers against the best interests of students. Again, certain students are more susceptible to these distorting effects. Others can cope relatively well with the maze of possibilities that confronts them. But it is very difficult to see this market either as an effective means of raising standards or increasing participation or creating a national 'culture of learning'.

Notes

1 ESRC Grant No L123251006, part of *The Learning Society Programme*.

2 Except of a mutually market-advantageous form.

3 While we were sociologically aware of the significance of 'race' in issues of urban education in the conceptualisation of our research, and this was a part of the construction of our student sampling and student interviews, we did not set out to highlight racial issues as opposed to class, gender or disability.

4 While we are highlighting 'race' specifically here, the market works in similar ways in relation to working-class students and some students with special needs, also within the 'economy of student worth' it gives some advantages to females. In practice, of course, class, race and gender are intercut and interrelated in patterns of worth, access, opportunity and discrimination.

5 There is a clear mismatch between the privatised Careers Service system of structures and targets and students' uncertainties and instabilities. They often seem to talk past one another.

6 These pressures are constantly increasing as schools strive to compete in local league tables. There is a massive malfunction here whereby concentration on key qualifications clashes directly with a major life-course decision.

7 We interviewed only a small number of parents in the first phase of the study, although many of the young people talked about the role their families played in their decision making, We will be interviewing more parents later in phase two.

References

Ainley, P. and Green, A. (1996) 'Missing the targets: the new state of post-16 education and training', *Forum*, vol 38, no 1, pp 22-3.

Bagley, C. (1996) 'Black and white unite or flight? The racialised dimension of schooling and parental choice', *British Educational Research Journal*, vol 22, no 5, pp 569-80.

Ball, S.J. (1998) 'Ethics, self interest and the market form in education', *Markets, Managers and Public Service?*, Occasional Paper No 1, London: Centre for Public Policy Research, King's College London.

Ball, S.J. and Vincent, C. (1998) 'I heard it on the grapevine: "hot" knowledge and school choice', *British Journal of Sociology of Education*, vol 19, no 4, pp 377-400.

Ball, S.J., Bowe, R.A. and Gewirtz, S. (1994) 'Competitive schooling: values, ethics and cultural engineering', *Journal of Curriculum and Supervision*, vol 9, no 4, pp 350-67.

Ball, S.J., Maguire, M. and Macrae, S. (1997) 'The post-16 education market: ethics, interests and survival', *BERA Annual Conference*, 11-14 September, University of York.

Ball, S.J., Macrae, S. and Maguire, M. (1998) 'Race, space and the further education marketplace', *Race, Ethnicity and Education*, vol 1, no 3, pp 171-89.

Banks, M., Bates, I., Breakwell, G., Bynner, J., Emler, N., Jamieson, L. and Roberts, K. (1992) *Careers and identities*, Buckingham: Open University Press.

Bartlett, W. and Le Grand, J. (1993) *Quasi markets and social policy*, London: Macmillan.

Bates, I. and Riseborough, G. (1993) 'Deepening divisions, fading solutions', in I. Bates, and G. Riseborough (eds) *Youth and inequality*, Buckingham: Open University Press.

Bynner, J., Ferri, E., Shepherd, P., Parsons, S., Joshi, H., Pierella, P., Smith, K., Montgomery, S., Schoon, I. and Wiggins, R. (eds) (1997) *Twenty-something in the 1990s: Getting on, getting by, getting nowhere*, Aldershot: Ashgate.

Cheng, Y. (1995) *Staying on in full-time education after 16: Do schools make a difference?*, London: DfEE.

Dearing, R. (1996) *Review of qualifications for 16-19 year olds*, London: SCAA.

Edwards, T., Fitz, J. and Whitty, G. (1989) *The state and private education: An evaluation of the assisted places scheme*, Lewes: Falmer.

Foskett, N.H. and Hesketh, A.J. (1996) *Student decision-making and the post-16 market place*, Southampton: Centre for Research in Education Marketing.

Fryer, B. (1997) *Learning for the twenty-first century*, National Advisory Group for Continuing Education and Lifelong Learning, London: DfEE.

Gewirtz, S., Ball, S.J. and Bow, R. (1993) 'Values and ethics in the marketplace: the case of Northwark Park', *International Journal of Studies in Education*, vol 3, no 2, pp 233-53.

Gewirtz, S., Ball, S.J. and Bow, R. (1995) *Markets, choice and equity in education*, Buckingham: Open University Press.

Gillborn, D. (1995) *Racism and anti racism in real schools*, Buckingham: Open University Press.

Goffman, E. (1971) *The presentation of self in everyday life*, Harmondsworth: Penguin.

Harvey, D. (1989) *The condition of postmodernity*, Oxford: Basil Blackwell.

Herbert, A. and Callender, C. (1998) *The funding lottery*, London: Policy Studies Institute.

Hodkinson, P., Sparkes, A.C. and Hodkinson, H. (1996) *Triumphs and tears: Young people, markets and the transition from school to work*, London: David Fulton.

Keith, M. and Cross, M. (eds) (1993) *Racism, the city and the state*, London: Routledge.

Kennedy, H. (1997) *Learning works: How to widen participation*, Coventry: FEFC.

Macrae, S. (1997) *Parents: Active participants or puzzled bystanders in the choice of post-16 education and training?*, London: King's College London.

Macrae, S., Maguire, M. and Ball, S.J. (1996) 'Opportunity knocks: "choice" in the post-16 education and training market', *Markets in Education: Policy, Process and Practice*, Heist: University of Southampton.

Macrae, S., Maguire, M. and Ball, S.J. (1997) *The role of grapevine knowledge in student decision-making*, London: King's College London.

Miles, R. (1989) *Racism*, London: Routledge.

NIACE (1996) *Creating two nations*, Leicester: Gallup.

OECD (1994) *School, a matter of choice*, Paris: OECD.

Reay, D. (1996) 'Contextualising choice: social power and parental involvement', *British Educational Research Journal*, vol 22, no 5, pp 581-96.

Reay, D. and Ball, S.J. (1997) 'Spoilt for choice: the working class and educational markets', *Oxford Review of Education*, vol 23, no 1, pp 89-101.

Rees, G., Fevre, R., Furlong, J. and Gorard, S. (1997) 'History, place and the learning society: towards a sociology of lifetime learning', *Journal of Education Policy*, vol 12, no 6, pp 485-98.

Roberts, K. (1993) 'Career trajectories and the mirage of increased social mobility', in I. Bates and G. Riseborough (eds) *Youth and inequality*, Buckingham, Open University Press.

Schagen, S., Johnson, F. and Simkin, C. (1996) *Sixth form options: Post-compulsory education in maintained schools*, Slough: NFER.

Solomos, J. (1993) 'The local politics of racial equality: policy innovation and the limits of reform', in M. Cross and M. Keith (eds) *Racism, the city and the state*, London: Routledge.

Thomas, A. and Dennison, B. (1991) 'Parental or pupil choice – who really decides in urban schools?', *Education Management and Administration*, vol 19, no 4, pp 243-51.

West, A. and Varlaam, A. (1991) 'Choosing a secondary school: parents of junior school children', *Educational Research*, vol 33, no 1, pp 22-30.

4

The costs of learning: the policy implications of changes in continuing education for NHS staff

Therese Dowswell, Bobbie Millar and Jenny Hewison

Introduction

The National Health Service is the largest employer in the UK, with a workforce of more than 900,000. Over the past two decades the service has undergone a major reorganisation. Under the Conservative government there was an attempt to separate the so-called purchasers of healthcare from the providers. In effect, the changes have resulted in what Le Grand and Bartlett (1993) have described as a 'quasi-market', with local hospital and community trusts providing healthcare services, and with health authorities purchasing services on behalf of their local populations. This organisational change has been mirrored by changes in the way that education is provided for healthcare staff. The delivery of healthcare education has largely shifted from provision in-house by larger hospitals to provision by universities. Professional development departments within hospital trusts still exist and such departments continue to provide non-accredited short courses for staff. However, the bulk of professional training at pre- and post-registration level for nursing and other professional staff is now provided within university departments. Thus, while two decades ago most nurse education would have been directly provided and funded within the NHS, now the purchaser and provider functions have been separated: the purchaser being the health service and the providers being higher education institutions (Humphreys and Quinn, 1994; Humphreys, 1996a). In some local areas, representatives from hospital trusts, GP fundholding practices and NHS Executive regional offices have formed consortia to coordinate the purchase of higher education courses (Humphreys, 1996b).

However, NHS consortia and purchasing authorities are not the only purchasers of courses for healthcare staff. A second group of purchasers of continuing education in the NHS comprises individual members of staff. The demand for continuing education by nurses and other healthcare staff is high. This is partly the result of national guidelines from the United Kingdom Central Council for Nursing Midwifery and Health Visiting (UKCC), which insist that to remain on the professional register (and to continue in clinical practice) staff must show evidence of participating in continuing education. At the moment, the recommendation for nurses is for a minimum of five study days every three years (UKCC, 1994).

While other professional groups (eg physiotherapists) are not covered by these regulations, there is a general sense among staff that they must participate in continuing education, and be seen to be doing so, to maintain their professional standing.

Other changes in nurse and midwifery education have also led to an increased demand for continuing education and training. Ten years ago, a major reform of nurse education was introduced in the

UK (UKCC, 1986). Prior to 1987, there were two strands of nurse education leading to two separate qualifications – to what have since become known as level one and level two nurses. The adoption of UKCC recommendations led to a phasing out of the level two qualification, and nurses with this qualification (enrolled nurses) were encouraged to upgrade their qualification to that of a level one nurse by engaging in a conversion course. Enrolled nurses made up a third of the nursing workforce in 1987. Meanwhile, training for level one nurses was to be upgraded to diploma level and student nurses were to have supernumerary status during their training. This change would obviously have serious effects in hospitals which had previously relied on student staff to provide services, and was thus phased in gradually (Humphreys, 1996a). The reforms also had implications for existing staff, and particularly for enrolled nurses, as conventional forms of training were to be replaced by new, more academic courses. The fact that reforms were likely to have a detrimental effect on staff already working in the service led to some opposition to the proposals from healthcare trade unions.

Currently, pre-registration training is being offered at diploma or advanced diploma levels. The purpose of the 1986 reforms was generally to upgrade nursing qualifications, to provide a single level of entry, and to create a single nursing qualification. However, in the short term the changes have resulted in a workforce whose members have undergone a variety of programmes of preparation and who possess a variety of qualifications. Nurses who trained more than five years ago following a conventional route will be less academically qualified than newly trained staff unless they have engaged in further education and training. Such changes are likely to exert considerable pressure on staff to upgrade their qualifications.

Hence, NHS community and hospital trusts have a strong interest in pre- and post-registration education in order to ensure that their workforce is maintained in terms of numbers and professional skills. However, qualified staff competing for jobs and promotion are also highly motivated to gain access to courses which provide academic qualifications. In this context, the question of how continuing education and training should be funded becomes highly controversial.

To summarise, the structure and funding of healthcare education is in transition. While two decades ago, all pre-registration training was funded and provided by the NHS, this is no longer the case. Further, the demand from individuals for courses that will allow them to upgrade their existing qualifications has increased significantly. From the point of view of a trust manager it may not be clear what the added value of such an upgrading is likely to be. From the point of view of an individual, an upgraded qualification may have value in the job market but may not necessarily enhance their job performance.

The study

We set out to explore some of these issues by interviewing participants attending a range of post-registration continuing education courses and NHS trust managers. In particular, we examined for a number of courses, how individuals were funded, whether they had release from work to undertake study and the effects of course participation on their home and working lives. In this chapter we concentrate on issues of release from work and funding. The effects of course participation on the lives of individuals have been discussed elsewhere (Dowswell et al, 1998).

Between February 1996 and July 1997, 89 healthcare staff participating in continuing education courses and a number of training managers from NHS trusts were interviewed.

The staff were attending a variety of courses, with a variety of funding mechanisms and modes of provision. Here we will illustrate this variety by focusing on three post-registration courses: a conversion course for enrolled nurses, a diploma level specialist course and a degree programme. Interviews with staff were recorded on audiotape and we illustrate views with extracts from interviews.

The conversion course

With changes in nurse education the enrolled nurse (EN) qualification has been phased out. Nevertheless, a large section of the workforce in the late 1980s possessed this qualification and conversion courses were introduced to allow these staff to upgrade. Such courses have been provided both full- and part-time and more recently via open learning methods. In our sample, we included 16 enrolled nurses in the process of converting their general nursing qualification via the *Nursing Times* Open Learning course. This was a two-year programme with attendance on approximately one day each month, and fortnightly for evening tutorial sessions, along with clinical placements lasting approximately six weeks. Students were recommended to spend approximately eight hours each week on course work.

The specialist diploma course

For many specialist areas within nursing (such as neonatal or intensive care) diploma level courses are available which have been validated by the English National Board for Nursing, Health Visiting and Midwifery (ENB). For a large number of these courses successful students are also awarded a specialist diploma and 80 or 90 credit accumulation and transfer (CAT) points. These courses may be provided full- or part-time. In our sample we included 19 students attending such courses, all of them attended full-time over six months. These courses are not compulsory but there is an expectation that nurses and midwives working in specialist areas will possess the relevant ENB qualification. For some specialist areas, such as neonatal nursing, there are national guidelines and targets on the desired ratio of staff with specialist training.

The degree course

While a degree level qualification is not required to practise as a nurse or midwife, our results indicate that many staff now feel that such qualifications are necessary in order to be employed at or above certain grades. For the 25 participants included in our sample this course required part-time attendance (two hours each week per module) as well as self-directed study of at least 4-5 hours per week, which students were expected to undertake outside taught time. Many students undertook two modules simultaneously and therefore doubled attendance and the recommended study time. The number of modules a student had to undertake to meet degree requirements varied and depended on

previous qualifications and accreditation of prior experiential learning (APEL). A typical student would attend for two years and would complete a total of 12 modules (two per term and six per year), equivalent to the third year of a traditional degree programme. The cost per module was £150 plus a course registration fee. Hence, the total cost of a two-year course would be in the region of £1,800.

The findings

Funding arrangements

For the specialist and conversion courses the issue of fees from the students' point of view was relatively straightforward. All of the students interviewed had had their fees paid by their employer under what are known as Working Paper 10 arrangements (DoH, 1989). Thus, a student attending a full-time neonatal course would have her basic salary paid by her employing trust, and in turn the trust would be reimbursed to cover staff replacement costs. In effect, however, despite full funding, attendance at a specialist course created major financial burdens for students. The basic salary paid during course attendance did not include any enhancements for working unsocial hours. So, while attending specialist courses, salaries were reduced by between £100-£200 per month if the student normally worked regular nights and weekends. In the quotations which follow, students describe the effects of this pay reduction:

> "The cut in salary has been an immense problem ... the financial costs have been immense. We have just bought a house and with the two kids and the nursery, the cut in salary has been really noticed." (Level one nurse)

> "The course costs you about £1,200 to go and do it because you are losing that much money in extra duty payments and stuff. So financially it is quite difficult to do it ... you don't get any financial reward for doing it when you have completed it." (Level one nurse)

For students participating in the degree programme, we identified a variety of funding arrangements. However, students were likely to bear most of the financial burden associated with course fees themselves. Of 25 students interviewed, approximately half (13) were paying the entire course fees themselves (an annual fee in the region of £900). Only one student was fully funded by her employer, while three students had at least 50% of the fees reimbursed by their employing trust. The remaining students had a smaller contribution to the course fees paid by their employer or had sought charitable aid.

The variety of funding arrangements was a source of resentment for many degree programme students and the salary reductions associated with attending the specialist courses created hardship for some. All of the students on all three courses identified a variety of other expenses associated with the course: travel, stationery and library costs. Some students paid for typing services and some bought word processing equipment to prepare written assignments themselves.

We identified three types of reactions by students to payment of fees:

- willing acceptance ("I am happy to pay the fees");
- stoicism ("I am prepared to pay if I must");
- resentment ("I think it's unfair and I'm unhappy about paying the fees/a contribution to the fees myself").

Of the 25 degree students interviewed 11 expressed resentment, nine stoicism and the remaining four acceptance (one was making no contribution). Not surprisingly, those paying most tended to be least happy. Twenty-two of the degree students thought that course fees should be shared between employees and employers. The rest felt that the full cost should be met by the employer. Examples are given below of the main types of reaction.

The acceptors

"I sort of realised we wouldn't get it [funding] ... but because I enjoy it and I feel as though I'm personally gaining from it, then I said I'd pay it." (Level one nurse)

"I'm not too bothered...I can pay. Luckily." (Level one nurse)

The stoics

"I don't mind too much in that I am doing it for myself, I'm not doing it for the trust. I'm taking the course for myself, but it's a little more upsetting when there's a couple of girls in my class at the moment, they're getting 75% funding and full study leave." (Level one nurse)

"Well, I suppose it is just the way things are these days. I expected it at the beginning so.... It is frustrating when you hear of other places, other hospitals ... that do give funding, but I think you just come to [the fact that] I wanted to do the course and anything that benefits me, I expected to pay it. People at work, a lot of people, think it is a lot of money to pay for a course. I suppose it is. I can think of better things to spend it on.... I feel that I am fortunate because I can afford to pay. There's a lot of people I know at work who would like to do further studying but they just can't afford the course fees." (Level one nurse)

The resenters

"I think it is unfair, but it is almost expected that you take up some further education if you want to get any further, but to not actually help you with that I do think is unfair. But that is the way it is. Which is wrong." (Level one nurse)

"Very bitter I tell you. I still feel, when I talk about it, I still get irate, because you just feel you have been used." (Level one nurse)

It was clear from student accounts that it was the variety in funding arrangements that was the main source of resentment rather than students being asked to contribute at all. The fact that the vast majority of degree students thought that shared funding arrangements were appropriate demonstrates this. The variety of funding arrangements was not simply due to different arrangements in different trusts. Within the same trust students were not guaranteed equitable treatment. Not surprisingly, those students on the conversion and specialist courses who were fully funded by their employers were much less likely to say that they were prepared to pay the fees themselves. They were also much more likely to say that they thought the employer was the most appropriate source of funding. While five of the enrolled nurses (of 16) thought that they might be willing to pay course fees, all of them thought that their own employer or the government *should* pay for the conversion course. All but one of the 19 specialist nurses interviewed similarly thought that they should not be called upon to pay fees. We quote here the one nurse who had doubts about this:

> "Well at one time, instinctively I feel like saying that the employer should pay, or the government or, you know, whoever. But I am not sure whether that is right or not. I mean there is no way I could [pay] ... but education is going like that anyway, and, you know, I sometimes wonder about my own children's further education. We'll have to pay for that. But on the other hand, if you are saying that people should pay, it does sort of limit the opportunities to people with, like, limited means. I'm not sure if that is right either." *(Level one nurse)*

Study leave

College recommendations for students attending the open learning conversion course were that students should have a minimum of 2.5 hours release from work each week, and that they should expect to devote approximately 8 hours each week on coursework. Of 16 students, seven received the minimum recommended study leave, two slightly more and seven less than 2.5 hours. Four students felt that the arrangements for leave were unfair, and irrespective of the amount of leave awarded, most students found it difficult to fit in the recommended amount of study. The effects of the course on students' home lives were particularly acute for this group.

Similarly, while students on the specialist course were released full-time for the course, the amount of work they were expected to complete in their own time was substantial. Students described spending between 8-20 hours per week of their own time on coursework. It is worth remembering that all of these students were mature, the youngest being 26. The sample was also predominantly female and these participants saw themselves as responsible for home and childcare. Two students describe their experience of studying outside course hours:

> "I would say it gets up to about three hours on an evening during the week and at least eight to ten hours on [my day off] and then at the weekends I'm doing say at least eight hours a day." *(Level one nurse)*

> "I spend most weekends studying because my husband will take the girls out and do things with them, and also in the evening, two hours on a night." *(Level two nurse)*

For the enrolled nurses this study time would be fitted around their normal shift work and it would not be unusual for a nurse to work a night after being up during the day.

> "I get up early, come to college and then go to work." *(Level one nurse)*

For the degree students, 16 had no study leave whatsoever. For the rest, seven individuals had negotiated up to half a day or less each week, while two had a full day release each week. Like fees, study time was a source of resentment, and the variable treatment was the main source of irritation.

> "To be perfectly honest [whether you get time off] seems to be whether your face fits and that is unfortunate. It is very surprising, study leave, if it is granted it is always given to senior members of staff." *(Level one nurse)*

Even where there was limited release it was sometimes given grudgingly. One student commented that she was allowed to leave work early in order to arrive in time for an evening tutorial session; in the following quotation she describes the attitude of her line manager:

> "I mean he was OK about sort of going off early but he still does say things like, 'Oh off you go again, leaving early', sort of thing. And what he is trying to tell us is that he still thinks we are doing this for our own benefit. You know, all right, we are sort of going from here at half past three, but we are not actually leaving college till nearly half past nine and it is really not an easy option to study part time. But it hasn't changed his attitude at all. He still feels as if he is doing us a major favour." *(Audiologist)*

The issue of study leave is complex. For degree course students, no staff replacement costs were available and decisions about leave were made informally by managers on wards. Thus, the opportunity to offer leave was limited. Within staffing budgets approximately 15% is built in to cover sick leave and training, but, while the demand for training has increased, the resources to pay for cover have not. Hence, cover for most students was a very informal affair, and if wards were particularly busy, or if staffing levels were strained due to sickness, release was not granted. In general, ward managers were fairly accommodating, arranging the staffing rota so that individuals could attend training events and peers would provide cover for colleagues, usually without ill feeling.

Where staff replacement costs were provided, they were not necessarily used to fund a replacement member of staff. In fact none of those interviewed thought that they had been replaced. Replacement costs tended to be absorbed into an overall staffing budget, so again, at the ward level cover was an informal affair. This informality would mean that cover arrangements were not straightforward; of the degree students, six identified specific difficulties with regard to cover. Either they were unable to negotiate a particular day off to attend the course in their own time, or the provision of cover for leave caused problems on the ward. Leaving a busy ward early to attend a course was not always easy, as the following extract shows:

> *"I find it difficult because I suppose I am always conscious of the amount of work that still needs to be done ... I don't think there is ever a right time to say, well I'm taking a couple of hours off here because I never get a lull." (Level one nurse)*

For training managers the questions of funding and release were difficult to resolve. The senior managers we interviewed all agreed that decisions about leave were usually made at the ward level and the consequences of releasing staff in terms of maintaining the service were therefore the responsibility of senior sisters and ward managers. The extract below illustrates that decisions about leave were not simple for ward staff and that managers frowned on any decisions which led to the need for extra staff to provide cover for staff attending training events.

> *"I have a principle that says that I will not support study leave with agency staff or overtime. So the team leader has got to make a judgement on, if this person has*

> *asked to go on study leave, can I manage to send him without any service implications? I say to them, that you have got to understand that the service comes first because it is the bread and butter.... I am saying to the team leaders, you know, you can do whatever you like so long as the service is covered. There have been occasions whereby ... such and such a team leader has asked for agency but she's got members of the team that are on study leave on that day, and that's really, that can be a conflict, because I will be saying to the team leader, no, well, you sort that out." (Senior Nurse Manager)*

Most managers avoided situations where patients were likely to suffer as a result of study leave. When asked about whether the service was ever compromised, managers were usually adamant that that would not be allowed to happen – the service comes first. In some areas such as theatres or intensive care, numbers could not be allowed to fall below a certain critical level without closure of a bed or a theatre session. Most recognised that maintaining quality was difficult.

> *"I mean obviously, you can't give the same quality of care if there are usually six of you on ... and on a particular day there's four. But, I think perhaps quality of care can sometimes be compromised. That decision is very much at the ward level and it's that person's responsibility to ensure that the ward is covered." (Senior Nurse Manager)*

The wider issue of whether particular courses should be funded by the trust or the employee was largely met with the response from managers – it depends on who benefits from the course.

> *"If I decide that I want somebody trained in something, then there's no doubt about it. It's the organisation [that] should pay for it. If the person comes to me themselves and wants to do something which I consider is not going to be to the benefit of this department, then I think we ought to be making some judgements then on whether they pay or we pay." (Senior Manager)*

These questions of who should pay for and who benefits from a particular course are by no means simple. We end this section with a longer extract from an interview with a senior nurse manager as she raised a number of issues about the funding of continuing education and about attitudes within nursing towards continuing professional development. For example, the question of whether a degree level qualification is essential for a nurse employed at a particular grade from the point of view of the employer (and thus, whether such qualifications should be funded by trusts) was a burning, practical issue:

"You know, there is very much the academia side now in nursing. That has just heightened everybody's awareness. And of course ... it has been stipulated through the Royal College of Nursing for instance, to do with clinical grading that there are expectations, or there are standards of education that they would expect somebody to achieve perhaps for getting a G grade post or an H grade post. You would expect now, certainly most, certainly G grades, which is the senior sisters or ward managers to have now, probably to have first degree education ... some [staff] have a real chip on their shoulder about it. You see, the thing at the moment, there's the Project 2000 nurses coming out with diploma level.... Some of us in the nursing profession, not that I am against advancement or education, think some of us are actually beginning, or actually doubting, because everybody seems to be going off and doing a degree, is the degree being devalued?... There's mainly this view that nursing has just gone too, too far really, education wise.... I'm interviewing this afternoon for a G grade post. In talking to other people who are more experienced than me in interviewing at that level, they consider that a very senior post and automatically look for evidence of further study. Probably to degree level. You know it's the most, it seems the most obvious thing. Now you will get some people who will sort of more rationally say, well look, this person has experience of this and this and this and hasn't got a degree."

This manager raises a number of issues which we will return to in the concluding sections. First, she points to the difficulties for nurse managers in balancing academic qualifications against practical experience. Second, she indicates that the increasing emphasis on academic qualifications is a source of resentment among nursing staff, with some staff wondering whether it had all "gone too far". Last, the issue of relating academic theory to clinical practice has long been a subject of debate for leaders of the nursing profession and NHS managers. These same issues were raised by most of the participants in our study.

Conclusions

The changes in nurse education and changes in the organisation of the health service mean that demand for continuing education by health service staff is sharply increasing. At the same time, funds for training have remained fairly constant. We recorded a number of instances where funding and leave arrangements were varied and informal, but the variety and informality have become sources of resentment. For many staff the principle of paying was not in itself objectionable, what was a problem was being asked to pay when others were not. An exception to this were the enrolled nurses who felt that their position was altered by the fact that their existing qualification had been devalued by changes in the overall structure of nurse training. All but one of these nurses were clear that they should not be asked to pay for their upgrade. Having said this, all of this group were expected to use their own time to undertake course work, as in most cases release from work fell far short of the actual hours required to complete it.

While few would dispute the fact that continual updating is essential for healthcare staff (and this has been recognised in national guidelines), the amount of continuing education that is necessary and the form that this should take are less clear. Trusts have a vested interest in funding education and training to ensure adequate staffing levels and safe and effective practice. Individuals also have a responsibility to practise their profession safely. However, over and above this, individuals in our sample frequently felt under pressure to train because qualifications were being used as a selection device for promotion, irrespective of whether a particular course would enhance job performance. As yet, there is very little evidence about the level of education necessary for competent job performance at any particular nursing grade. The science of measuring the links between educational level and job performance in nursing is still in its infancy (Fitzpatrick et al, 1993, 1994).

In one of the trusts where managers were interviewed, there was an attempt being made to identify the appropriate contribution of the trust to course fees for different types of course. However, whether or not a course was relevant to the business of the trust was decided at the ward level by many different nurse managers rather than being a matter of policy at the trust level. Before it is possible, then, to answer the question of who should fund continuing education for healthcare staff, it is necessary to step back and examine the question of what sort and what amount of training are necessary to ensure that staff perform well. We hope that other research taking place as part of *The Learning Society Programme* will answer some of these questions. Meanwhile, many healthcare staff feel that they are being asked to shoulder responsibility for their training without adequate support.

Policy implications

The debate concerning the funding of pre- and post-registration education of healthcare staff is part of the wider policy debate concerning the funding of higher education (Dearing Report, 1997). At the same time, the healthcare workforce is a 'special case' for a number of reasons. First, the NHS is funded from the public purse and is the largest employer in the UK. The service employs almost a million individuals, and the nursing workforce alone costs the taxpayer in excess of £8 billion per year. If the taxpayer was to foot the bill for a general upgrading of a workforce of this size, the cost is likely to be high. While no one would dispute that maintaining levels of competence to ensure safe practice is a legitimate use of tax revenue, whether the government should support the more general education of qualified nursing staff is more questionable. It is certainly not clear that the current Labour government supports the idea that nursing should move towards being an all-graduate profession (Castledine, 1998).

The issues of education and training are closely linked with those of recruitment and retention of staff and this is reflected in the pre-registration funding of nurse education. Unlike other entrants into higher education, nursing students fall outside the Dearing recommendations regarding funding and are fully funded via a bursary paid by the health service. If nurse preparation is indeed general education, there may be a case for insisting that student nurses should shoulder some of the cost of their education and/or maintenance. However, in practice, it is proving difficult to recruit nursing students even with the relatively generous bursary

paid to students. Indeed there have been serious concerns that at present levels of recruitment the service will face a staffing crisis by 2010. The ageing of the existing nursing workforce is exacerbating these problems (*The Guardian*, 1998).

As far as continuing education of NHS staff is concerned, while generous study leave provision may act as a motivational force to encourage participation and may assist in staff retention, it is also necessary for educational provision to be perceived as intrinsically worthwhile. The staff we interviewed did not always view education in this light. Gaining a degree, for example, was not generally regarded as a means of improving current practice. Professional organisations may promote the idea that nursing should become an all-graduate profession, but unless the rank and file workforce agree and unless employers support this move, the recommendations of professional organisations are empty rhetoric. Unless there are clear national guidelines from nursing organisations which are fully backed and supported by employers, then there is likely to be inequitable treatment as regards leave and fees. If employers do not think that degree level qualifications are necessary, then this needs to be clear. Using a qualification as a vague 'proxy' measure of competence (especially when this is not done explicitly) leaves staff feeling confused and resentful and may undermine their confidence in their existing skills and knowledge. We found evidence that this was occurring in our study.

At present there is no single policy message from employers and professional organisations. Nurses do not seem to understand UKCC guidelines on continuing education and the onus is on individuals rather than employers to take responsibility for continuing education. This emphasis on individual responsibility for learning has been in tune with the previous Conservative government's policy on continuing education (DoH, 1995). Having said this, our study showed that at the local level, employers did support continuing education in practical ways. However, the level of support varied considerably. This local variation in support for learning will mean that continuing education is as much a matter of chance as management. A policy framework developed at government level, supported by professional organisations, healthcare unions and employers, would mean that lifelong learning for staff was managed to ensure equity and efficiency in the continuing education of health service staff.

References

Castledine, G. (1998) 'Value of higher education to the nursing profession', *British Journal of Nursing*, vol 7, no 18, p 1130.

Dearing Report (1997) *Report of the National Committee of Inquiry into Higher Education*, London: DfEE.

DoH (Department of Health) (1989) *Working for patients: Education and training*, Working Paper 10, London: HMSO.

DoH (1995) *Career pathways: Nursing, midwifery and health visiting*, London: HMSO

Dowswell, T., Hewison, J. and Millar, B. (1998) 'Enrolled nurse conversion: trapped into training', *Journal of Advanced Nursing*, vol 28, no 3, pp 540-7.

Fitzpatrick, J.M., While, A.E. and Roberts, J.D. (1993) 'The relationship between nursing and higher education', *Journal of Advanced Nursing*, vol 18, pp 1488-97.

Fitzpatrick, J.M., While, A.E. and Roberts, J.D. (1994) 'The measurement of nurse performance and its differentiation by course participation', *Journal of Advanced Nursing*, vol 20, pp 761-8.

Humphreys, J. (1996a) 'English nurse education and reform of the National Health Service', *Journal of Education Policy*, vol 11, pp 655-79.

Humphreys, J. (1996b) 'Education commissioning by consortia: some theoretical and practical issues relating to qualitative aspects of British nurse education', *Journal of Advanced Nursing*, vol 24, pp 1288-99.

Humphreys, J. and Quinn, F.M. (1994) *Health care education: The challenge of the market*, London: Chapman and Hall.

Le Grand, J. and Bartlett, W. (eds) (1993) *Quasi-markets and social policy*, London: Macmillan.

The Guardian (1998) 'In search of their other half', 15 July, p 21.

UKCC (1986) *Project 2000: A new preparation for practice*, London: UKCC.

UKCC (1994) *The future of professional practice: The Council's standards for education and practice following registration*, London: UKCC.

5

Skill trends in Britain: trajectories over the last decade[1]

Alan Felstead, David Ashton, Brendan Burchell and Francis Green

Introduction

"Learning and skills are critical to UK competitiveness and the Government is committed to raising standards of achievement to match the best in the world". (Gillian Shephard, then Secretary of State for Education and Employment, DfEE, 1996a, p 2)

"Learning is the key to prosperity – for each of us as individuals, as well as for the nation as a whole. Investment in human capital will be the foundation of success in the knowledge-based economy of the twenty-first century.... We cannot rely on a small elite, no matter how highly educated or highly paid. Instead, we need the creativity, enterprise and scholarship of all our people." (David Blunkett, current Secretary of State for Education and Employment, DfEE, 1998, p 7).

It appears to be a commonly and widely held view in government circles that skills and learning have an important bearing on the competitiveness of British business, and hence on the economic wealth and prosperity of the nation. Similar pronouncements can also be heard in European policy-making discourse (eg, European Commission, 1994, ch 7) as well as in global overviews carried out by institutions such as the International Labour Organisation (ILO, 1998). Behind these pronouncements is the notion that private capital is becoming increasingly able to locate particular parts of its business in different countries across the globe. The absence or presence of a skilled workforce is claimed to be one of the crucial factors likely to determine where capital decides to locate its most prestigious, high productivity, high pay and technologically advanced parts.

However, rhetorical statements of the kind outlined above only get us so far. The acid test is whether it is possible to detect practical policies designed to give skills and learning greater emphasis in practice. As far as Britain is concerned there are several actions and initiatives which have been formulated with just such an aim in mind. The National Targets for Education and Training, for example, were launched in 1991, with the intention of putting Britain at least on a par with those of competitor countries. Following a period of consultation they were revised and updated in 1995. They are currently (1998) being reviewed for a second time. Although based mainly on exhortation, the Targets have been used to structure and guide decisions over which government has an influence. The funding of Training and Enterprise Councils (TECs) has been partly influenced by the progress individual TECs are making towards achievement of the Targets in their area (see Felstead, 1994, 1998).

Monitoring of how Britain compares with competitor nations has also been given greater emphasis. The government's Skills Audit, for example, remains a key source on which policy makers evaluate how Britain's skills compare with France, Germany, the US and Singapore (DfEE and Cabinet Office, 1996; Steedman, 1997). This confirms the well known but worrying finding that while Britain produces proportionately more graduates than most of its competitor economies, the nation lags a long way behind its competitors as far as intermediate level qualifications are concerned (cf Steedman et al, 1991; Prais, 1993). Important though these findings are, workforce skills in this context are simply read off from the proportions holding qualifications at a particular level (see Felstead, 1996, 1997). However, such narrowness (and seeming simplicity) does have its merits. There are, for example, many reliable data sources available for qualification attainment ranging from the awarding bodies to large sample surveys of the population. Many of these data sources have been collected on a consistent basis over time and hence make trend analysis possible.

However, there is a growing realisation that qualifications data alone is a crude measurement instrument. Policy interest in what were originally called 'core skills', now referred to as 'key skills', has been influential in recent government thinking and is currently helping to reshape Britain's system of qualifications. These refer to skills which employers are increasingly demanding as a result of the changing nature of work. Problem solving, computing skills and numeracy are said to be increasingly required as a result of technological change in the workplace. Furthermore, if workers are being given more and more scope to organise their work, empowered or required to take on multiple tasks, the importance of problem-solving skills is accentuated still further and increased emphasis is placed on self-improvement through learning. Similarly, with the delayering of management it is frequently argued that workers have to communicate more with each other, or with clients or suppliers, and become self-directed learners.

From a research perspective the emphasis placed on key skills in policy making begins to broaden the conception of skills. However, existing knowledge on skill trends is still restricted to skills as proxied by the qualifications individuals hold or the length of schooling received, as the following section will reveal. The aim of this chapter is to widen the debate by comparing the results of two surveys – one carried out in 1986, the other carried out in 1997. Inevitably, the validity of this procedure rests on the assumption that both datasets are representative of the British working population. This chapter, therefore, briefly considers this issue, and draws attention to the differences and similarities that exist between the two datasets as well as the methods used to compare skills over time. More substantively, the chapter examines skill

trends over the 1986-97 period along a number of dimensions. These include the qualifications individuals would now require to get their current job, the qualifications they actually use at work, the length of training required for the job and time needed to learn to do the job well. The chapter concludes that the trajectory of skill trends over the last decade has been consistently in the upward direction irrespective of the skill dimension chosen. Furthermore, women have seen their skill levels increase at a much faster rate than men's, thereby closing the skills gap between the sexes.

Existing knowledge

The *New Oxford Dictionary of English* defines 'skill' as "the ability to do something well", while the related term 'skilled' is defined as "having or showing the knowledge, ability, or training to perform a certain task or activity well" (Pearsall, 1998, p 1745). Despite this relatively clear definition there are several (competing) ways in which skill can be measured. One way is to examine the extent to which individuals are able to perform their work tasks without management interference. This method takes its cue from the sociological debates on the labour process prompted by the work of Braverman (1974). Another way draws its inspiration from occupational psychology. It measures skill according to what tasks people do in their jobs and how effectively they carry them out (Ash, 1988; Primoff and Fine, 1988). The third method is more economistic in its outlook since it seeks to measure an individual's stock of human capital endowments (eg, Becker, 1964; Stevens, 1994). This approach comes closest to the data reported on in this chapter (although elsewhere we examine skills drawing on other perspectives – see Green et al, 1999; Felstead et al, 1999).

It would be misleading to suggest that data on skill trends are simply not available to policy makers. However, the evidence on offer is narrow and restrictive. The most commonly used yardstick measures the educational attainment of the workforce. Taking this as the benchmark it is easy to conclude that skills have moved in the upward direction over the last decade or so – indeed the same is true for much of the 20th century. For example, one can point to staying-on rates after the compulsory leaving age which have risen substantially since the mid-1980s: the proportion of 16- to 18-year-olds in full-time education was only one in three in 1985/86, but by 1995/96 it rose to over one in two. Similarly, the proportions of 19- to 20-year-olds in higher education more than doubled from 12% to 27% over the same period (DfEE, 1996b). Qualifications data also point in the same upward direction. By the mid-1990s some sort of qualification was held by 80% of the working population compared with 63% a decade or so earlier. The proportion of degree holders rose from 7% to 12% during the same period. Thus both the flow and the stock of qualifications held in Britain have been steadily rising over the last decade. However, some researchers (eg, Green and Steedman, 1997) have pointed out that some of the newly emerging economies are raising the standards and schooling of their labour market entrants at a much faster rate than Britain's, hence narrowing the gap in the stock of qualifications between countries.

Despite the fact that policy makers have put much faith in raising participation rates and qualification attainment, doubts remain about whether they really do signal an upward movement in the skills of the British workforce. Increasing the workforce's ability to do more complex and difficult tasks does not mean that these skills are used at work. After all, it is often argued that some part of the skills problem facing Britain has been a deficiency of demand for high skilled labour, born out of strategic decisions made by British businesses to concentrate on comparatively low value added processes and products which demand low levels of skill and are rewarded with low pay (Keep and Mayhew, 1996; Ashton and Green, 1996).

Robinson and Manacorda (1997) provide evidence in support of this argument. Based on data contained in the Labour Force Survey in 1984 and 1994, they argue that the rise in qualifications says nothing about changing job requirements but instead gives employers the opportunity to recruit better qualified workers. The data show that increased qualifications are not concentrated in occupations or sectors thought to have rising skill requirements, but rather are spread relatively evenly across the workforce. Robinson and Manacorda (1997) also review a number of case studies which provide little evidence of employers consciously

raising the qualifications criteria for recruitment to jobs which demand more of those employed. However, the analysis they present is open to a number of potential objections. One problem is that case studies are limited in scope and that survey evidence is best placed to tackle the issue of credentialism (see later). Secondly, if technological innovation and changing forms of work organisation are fairly widespread and have a link with the skills required of workers (see Ashton and Felstead, 1998), one might expect qualifications to be evenly spread if they were being used to meet rising skills demand. Finally, there are significant measurement problems with the Labour Force Survey qualifications data on which the Robinson and Manacorda (1997) study relies (Bradley et al, 1997). For these reasons, one must remain cautious about whether the general rise in qualifications reflects an upskilling of work in Britain.

Another way of examining the trajectory of skills is to look at the changing nature of work in Britain. Rising proportions of non-manual workers have sometimes been taken as indicating an upward movement in skill levels. It is commonly known, for example, that there are many more managers in the workforce today than there were a decade or so ago. However, the similarly well known fact that craft workers have fallen significantly in recent years appears to have made little impact on the overall upward trend in the occupational profile of most advanced industrialised economies of the world. Despite these trends, many social scientists are uneasy about relying on occupational profiles as a measure of skill trends. After all, occupations themselves are not immune from change – while occupational titles themselves may remain unchanged for years, even decades, job content may be radically altered in ways which necessitate higher or lower skills. For example, some non-manual jobs are now little more than routine, requiring low skill levels and resembling traditional manual work in many respects. This prompts us to look beyond occupational labelling to the content of the job itself.

This approach was adopted in the Social Change and Economic Life Initiative (SCELI) and the Employment in Britain (EIB) surveys. Each asked individual respondents whether they thought their work skills had increased or decreased or remained the same compared to their job five years ago (Gallie, 1991, 1996). According to SCELI – carried out in 1986 – 52% of individuals experienced an increase in their skills, while only 9% reported a fall. A similar pattern was found six years later by EIB – 63% reported an increase, while just 9% reported a decline. In both surveys there appeared to be widespread upskilling within most occupational categories. However, this approach requires individuals to judge change, thereby opening up the measure to upward bias as individuals exaggerate increases and downplay decreases simply on account of self-esteem. Moreover, the changing nature of skills used at work may be misinterpreted by individuals as representing a change in skill levels. This evidence of upskilling, therefore, requires corroboration from other methods less prone to upward biases of this type. Some of this corroboration has already been possible by comparing the results of SCELI and EIB along a number of skill dimensions (see Gallie and White, 1993, ch 2). However, this chapter aims to update this analysis by comparing 1986 with the position in 1997.

Skills survey: trend analysis

In the months of January-May 1997 a major new survey of employed people in Britain was carried out – the Skills Survey (SS). Its purpose was to examine the skills of a representative sample of the employed British population. The questionnaire examined skill from a number of angles including the qualifications and training required for the job, how important particular job activities were, self-assessed competence in each activity and questions about the respondent's job five years ago. The interview also included a range of standard labour market and demographic questions. The dataset provides unique insights into the social construction of 'skill'. In particular, it can be used to determine whether conventional proxies provide an adequate measure of what tasks jobs entail and how effectively these are carried out; the relationship between various types of skills and economic rewards (see Green, 1998); and the link between organisational characteristics and skill formation (see Ashton and Felstead, 1998). However, several other features were also incorporated into its design. One of these

features was the capability of measuring skills trends over time – the substance of this chapter[2].

SS was designed to include SCELI-style questions on skills, accompanying prompts, use of show cards and response sets. These were identified and replicated word for word as far as possible. Several questions came under this rubric (see Appendix to this chapter). These included questions on the qualifications respondents had, what qualifications they would now require to get the same job and how useful these qualifications would be in doing the job. While qualifications held is a useful measure of the skills brought to the job by the individual, it is rather the level of qualification both required and necessary to do the job that is a closer measure of the actual skill involved in the job. Respondents were also asked about the length of training they had received for the type of work that they were doing and how long it had taken (or would take) them to learn to do the job well. Interpretation of the latter is open to a degree of ambiguity since it could be argued that a better educated person would be able to learn to do some jobs well more quickly than a person with less education. Alternatively, if the job called for manual dexterity, then it could be argued that the better educated would be slower learners since they may have put more emphasis on the development of cognitive abilities at the expense of manual skills. Less weight is therefore attached to responses generated from this question, although it provides a useful complement to the other skill measures. The results reported in this chapter are based on the responses generated by these questions[3].

Inevitably, comparing the results from one dataset with the results generated from another rests on the assumption that in so doing one is comparing a picture of Britain in 1986 with a picture of Britain 11 years later. It is important therefore to acknowledge readily the differences between the two datasets – of which there are many – and assess their impact on the validity of the comparison. To do otherwise could put the veracity of the findings in doubt (see Lloyd, 1997, p 38).

The aims of the two datasets differed considerably. SCELI's aims were much wider. It consisted of several surveys, although only one was concerned with work. This covered a range of issues, including people's past work careers, their current experience of employment or unemployment, attitudes to trade unionism, work motivation, broader sociopolitical values, and the financial position of the household. Clearly, this took it far beyond the much narrower concerns of SS. However, this does nothing to invalidate extracting common variables from each of the datasets and pooling them to produce another which contains an additional variable indicating the year the data were collected.

SCELI also had a wider focus than SS since it aimed to collect data on the workforce as a whole rather than on those in employment alone. In other words, SCELI included the unemployed in its scope, whereas SS did not. However, for the purposes of this chapter, this difference is of little relevance since the skills questions were only asked of those in work. As a result, the pooled dataset only contains information on the employed workforce and, since both surveys restricted the sample to include individuals of a certain age, they are all aged 20-60.

The geographical coverage of the two datasets requires comment. SCELI was based on data from six labour markets – Aberdeen, Coventry, Kirkcaldy, Northampton, Rochdale and Swindon. All, apart from Aberdeen, represented a travel-to-work area, a geographical area in which most of the population worked and lived (Turok, 1997; Coombes et al, 1997; Webster, 1997). The six areas were "selected to provide contrasting patterns of recent and past economic change" rather than being necessarily representative of Britain in 1986 (Gallie, 1994, p 336). SCELI was based on a random selection of addresses taken from the electoral registers in each of these areas, with probabilities proportional to the number of registered electors at the address. One eligible individual at each address was then interviewed at random. Three quarters (76%) of all eligible individuals selected for interview took part in the survey.

For SS, however, more complicated procedures were adopted in order to produce a representative sample of the employed workforce across Britain. First, a sample of 8,500 Postal Address Files (PAFs) in England, Wales and Scotland (south of the Caladeonian canal) was selected. Second, a list of all postal districts was generated and these were put into two groups – one for England and Wales and

one for Scotland – and sorted into regions and sub-regions. The resulting groupings were stratified according to their socioeconomic profile and levels of unemployment. A total of 10 postal districts were then drawn from the Scottish list using a random start and a predetermined sampling interval. The same method was used to derive a total of 90 postal districts from the English and Welsh list. In each of the selected postal districts, one postal sector (ie, PAF) was selected randomly (with probability proportional to the number of addresses). Finally, every 11th address was extracted from each PAF until a total of 85 addresses had been drawn. Individuals at each address were screened by Social and Community Planning Research (SCPR) interviewers according to the criteria for eligibility, with one eligible individual per address being randomly selected for interview. Of those selected for interview, 67% took part, with the main reason for not taking part being refusal.

Once pooled, the dataset contained a total of 6,514 cases, of which 4,047 (62%) were from SCELI and 2,467 (38%) from SS. However, before the analysis could begin we had to recode some of the variables as a result of changes in coding conventions between 1986 and 1997. For the 1986-92 comparison to proceed, the SCELI data had to be recoded according to the present-day Standard Occupational Classification (SOC) system[4]. Given the difference between classification systems such a mapping process can never be exact. However, the differences are relatively minor and can be ignored especially as the analysis we present in this chapter is based at the broad nine category level. Similarly, the industry data had to be recoded according to the latest classification system – Standard Industrial Classification (SIC92). SCELI had been coded according to the previous available system (SIC80). This recoding procedure, too, can never be exact. However, the differences are relatively minor and can be ignored for the purposes of this chapter since we pitch our analysis at the highest level of aggregation (CSO, 1993; OPCS, 1995, para 5.6).

What consequences, then, do these differences have for the representativeness of the two datasets? Is SCELI representative of Britain in 1986 and is SS reflective of Britain 11 years later? This issue has already been covered by several authors in the case of SCELI (eg, Marsh and Vogler, 1994, pp 59-60;

Gallie, 1996, p 134). Despite being based on six different local labour markets the evidence suggests that SCELI adds up to a picture which looks remarkably similar to the broader British picture in 1986. So, for example, the age, ethnicity, employment status, occupational and industrial profile of SCELI respondents is broadly in line with national estimates for 1986 (drawn from the Quarterly Labour Force Survey – see Ashton et al, 1999). Similarly, comparison of SS with national estimates for 1997 suggest much the same. However, both samples over-represent women. The data reported here has therefore been weighted to correct for this effect and the greater probability individuals in smaller households stand of being selected for interview and vice versa. We can be confident, therefore, that comparing the responses given to the same questions posed by SCELI in 1986 with SS in 1997 can be used to track skill trends in Britain over the last decade.

Skill trends over the last decade

For the purposes of this chapter, we have limited ourselves to five particular aspects of skill: qualifications held by respondents; qualifications required to get the type of job respondents now have; whether these credentials are relevant to the job itself; the time respondents spent training to do their current type of work; and the time taken to do the job well. Here, we have chosen to present the findings on each of these aspects rather than constructing a composite index or homing in on one particular indicator alone. Instead our aim in this chapter is to build up a consistent picture – drawing from a range of skill indicators – of the trajectory of skills in Britain over the last decade or so.

Qualifications held

The last decade has seen a renewed interest and vigorous debate surrounding the notion that Britain has undergone a skills revolution. The aggregate data for the late 1980s to early 1990s tend to confirm that this has indeed occurred. This has certainly been the main message of academic work and media reports of previous research in this area (eg, Gallie, 1991; Gallie and White, 1993; *Financial Times*, 1993). Our results suggest that this process – as we shall see – has extended well into the late

1990s. For example, workers in 1997 were more qualified than they were in 1986. Some 28% of those in work in 1986 had no qualifications compared to 19% of SS respondents surveyed just over a decade later[5]. This finding is entirely to be expected given our existing knowledge of rising staying-on rates among young people and the growth in qualifications held by existing members of the employed workforce as regularly monitored and published by government agencies such as the National Advisory Council for Education and Training Targets (NACETT, 1997). This raises the question of whether skill increases are the result of better qualified cohorts entering the labour market. This question is returned to later in the chapter when we consider the pattern of skill change by age (see below).

Qualifications required

While a useful first step in the measurement of skills, qualifications held do not indicate, except indirectly and with possible inaccuracy, the skills demanded at work. A better measure of the skill demanded of job holders is the qualification level that new recruits are required to have to get their jobs. On this measure, jobs appear to have become more demanding over the last decade. Fewer individuals in 1997 than in 1986 reported that no qualifications were needed to get the type of jobs they had, while more reported needing 'high level' (anything above A-level) qualifications. Whereas 62% of jobs required at least some qualifications in 1986, by 1997 this proportion had risen to 69%. For 'high level' qualifications the proportion rose from 20% to 24%. In fact, skill requirements rose at all levels of highest qualification, apart from National Vocational Qualification (NVQ) Level 3 where they fell slightly from 1986 to 1997 (see Figure 1).

Credentialism and qualifications 'used'

In this chapter we distinguish between 'credentialism' and 'over-education', although the literature often confuses the two. Credentialism, as discussed here, refers to the situation where employers – possibly as a sifting device – raise the qualification requirements for recruitment in the absence of a comparable rise in job demands[6]. Over-education, on the other hand, refers to a situation where individuals possess qualifications in

Figure 1: Qualifications required (1986 and 1997)

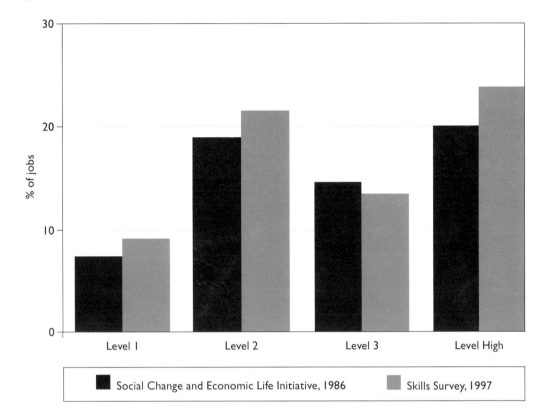

Notes: highest qualification level, ranked by NVQ equivalents. 'Level High' refers to everything above (NVQ Level 3, ie, A-level), 'Level 3' is roughly equivalent to A-level, 'Level 2' roughly equivalent to GCSE grades A-C, and 'Level 1' to GCSE grades D and below. All qualifications were precisely matched between surveys.

In this and subsequent figures, the data have been weighted by a factor determined by the number of eligible respondents at each address surveyed and by a factor which corrects for the slight over-representation of women in the raw samples.

Source: Social Change and Economic Life Initiative, 1986; Skills Survey, 1997

excess of those required to get the job irrespective of the demands of their work tasks, that is, what some prefer to call 'over-qualification'. While over-education has been quite widely studied (eg, Sloane et al, 1995), credentialism as defined here has received scant attention. To investigate the issue, SS respondents were asked to indicate on a four-point scale how necessary were the qualifications, which were required of new recruits, to do the job. Increasing credentialism would be indicated by a decline in the necessity of qualifications for doing the job between the observation points of 1986 and 1997.

Despite anecdotal evidence to the contrary, our data suggest little evidence of rising levels of credentialism by employers. Indeed, the largest movement is indicative of a decline in credentialism – for those jobs recruiting at NVQ Level 2 (equivalent of GCSE grades A*-C) the extent to which that qualification is judged 'essential' or 'fairly necessary' rose significantly, from 65% to 72% of job holders at that level. At other levels, small (non-significant) falls were recorded in the perceived necessity to do the job of the qualifications required for recruitment (see Figure 2).

Figure 2: Required qualifications necessary (1986 and 1997)

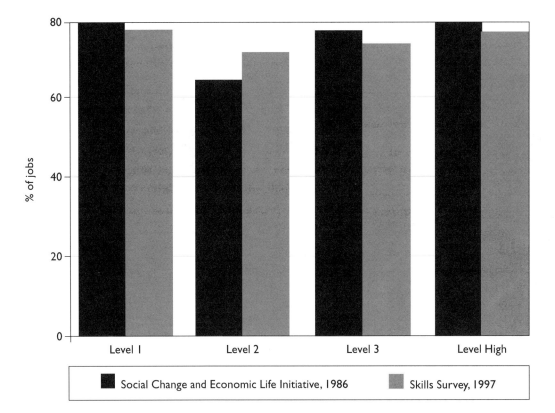

Source: Social Change and Economic Life Initiative, 1986; Skills Survey, 1997

Another measure of skills is to combine the answers on qualifications required to get jobs with the degree to which they are regarded as necessary for effective performance once in post. We term this as skills 'used' in a job and define it as the level of qualification which is both required of new recruits and either regarded as 'essential' or 'fairly necessary' to do the job. Measured on this score, there appears to have been a significant increase in skills over the period: the proportions in jobs 'using' degree level skills rose significantly from 8% in 1986 to 11% in 1997, the most rapid increases being recorded for women – a feature to which we will return later (see Figure 3). This suggests that rising qualification requirements to get jobs is not simply a case of pure credentialism by employers but is reflective of the changing nature of jobs themselves.

Over-education

Over-education occurs when individuals are in jobs for which they hold qualifications in excess of those demanded by employers for recruitment. Hence, a rise in over-education occurs when the gap between supply and demand widens. As in the case of credentialism, a key policy question is whether the rising supply of qualifications is being matched by rising employer demand or whether British workers are becoming over-qualified for the jobs they do. Our data allows us to address this question. We examine the proportions of those holding qualifications of a particular level for whom lower level qualifications would be sufficient to get the job in 1986 and compare these figures with those for 1997.

From the data reported in this chapter as well as from other data sources (eg, NACETT, 1997) we know that the proportions of workers holding qualifications of one sort or another has risen over the period. We also know that this increase is broadly in line with the rise in the proportion of jobs for which some qualifications are required for entry (cf Figure 1). It therefore comes as little surprise that there has been a small but insignificant fall in the extent of over-education among those

Figure 3: Degrees 'used' in job (1986 and 1997)

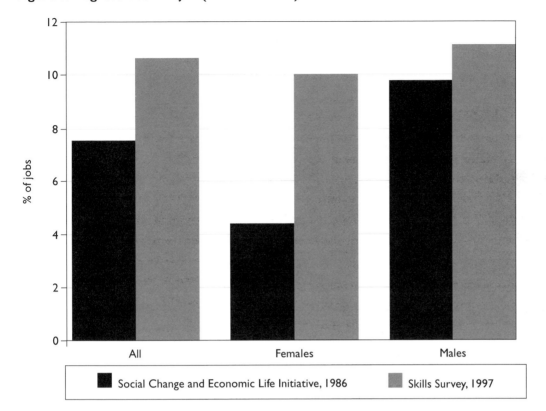

Source: Social Change and Economic Life Initiative, 1986; Skills Survey, 1997

with qualifications (see Figure 4). Little change in over-education is similarly detectable elsewhere in the qualification hierarchy. Among degree holders, for example, there has only been a small (statistically insignificant) rise in over-education. Nevertheless, in both 1986 and 1997 about three out of 10 degree holders were in jobs for which degrees were not an entry requirement. On this evidence, it might be argued that while the situation has not got markedly worse over the last decade, the overall level of employer demand for degrees remains persistently low. There were, at the same time, many workers without degrees in jobs that now require degrees of new recruits. The overall picture is therefore one of continuing poor matching of the supply and demand for degree qualifications.

Training time and learning time measures

The chapter has so far concentrated on various qualification-based measures of skill. Comparison of SCELI and SS also allows us to examine skill from a number of other angles. These include the time spent training for the type of work respondents do and the time spent learning to do the job well. The response sets for each of these questions consisted of a range of time-bound options. For the purposes of presentation we examine the proportions reporting 'short' and 'long' training/learning times, that is, the extremes of the spectrum. Figures 5 and 6 display the results of a focus on the length of time spent training for the type of work respondents do. This suggests an upward movement in skill over the 1986-97 period – the proportion of workers reporting 'short' training times (less than month) fell from 46% to 37%, while those reporting 'long' training times (over two years) rose from 22% to 29%. Both changes are statistically significant.

Figure 4: Over-education

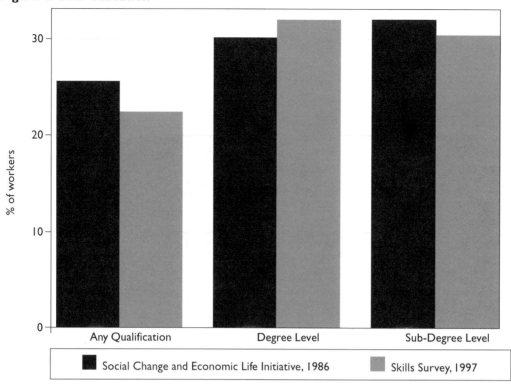

Note: 'Degree Level' refers to degrees; 'Sub-Degree Level' means any of: HNC/HND, or SHNC/SHND, or a nursing qualification (eg, SRN, SEN), or a teaching or other professional qualification (eg, law, medicine); and 'Any Qualification' refers to any qualification at all including degrees and sub-degrees.

Source: Social Change and Economic Life Initiative, 1986; Skills Survey, 1997

Figure 5: Under one month's training required

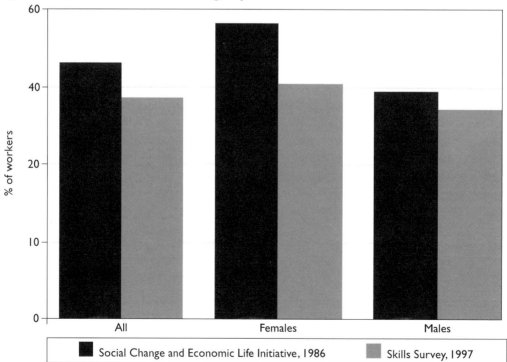

Source: Social Change and Economic Life Initiative, 1986; Skills Survey, 1997

Figure 6: Over two years' training required

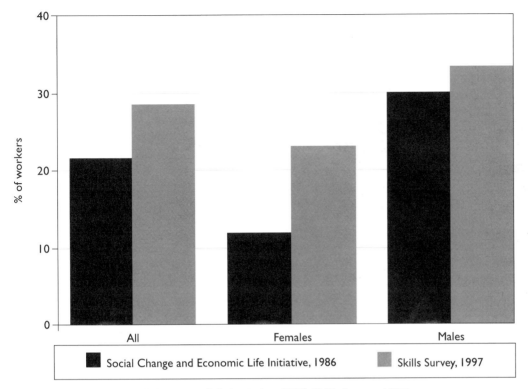

Source: Social Change and Economic Life Initiative, 1986; Skills Survey, 1997

Pattern by gender

Previous research has focused much attention on whether skills are becoming more polarised. Despite the fact that our evidence suggests an overall pattern of upskilling during the last decade, do particular groups of workers such as women experience faster rates of upskilling than others? As far as gender is concerned our data exhibits a consistent pattern in which women's skills are increasing at a much faster rate than men's, hence closing the gender gap. This has already been shown in many of the figures. Although women remain behind men on all of the skill indicators reported in this chapter, they have caught up substantially over the last decade. In 1997, for example, 71% of men's jobs required some qualifications on entry, up a little from 69% in 1986.

A similar, albeit less striking, pattern is evident for learning times. The proportion of respondents who judged that their jobs took a 'short' time to learn to do well (less than one month) fell significantly from 27% in 1986 to 21% in 1997. However, the proportion who suggested that their jobs took more

than two years to learn to do well did not significantly change over the period remaining at about 24% throughout.

A similar picture emerges from the other skill indicators examined in this chapter. The proportion of women in jobs that require a short training period or are relatively quick to pick up have fallen faster than the proportion of men in jobs with similarly low skill attributes. On the other hand, indicators of high skilled jobs such as long training periods and lengthy periods of experiential learning have risen faster among women than men. As a result, the gender gap between men's and women's jobs at both ends of the skills spectrum has narrowed (cf Figures 5-9). Nonetheless, a gap in men's favour remains.

Figure 7: Under one month's learning time

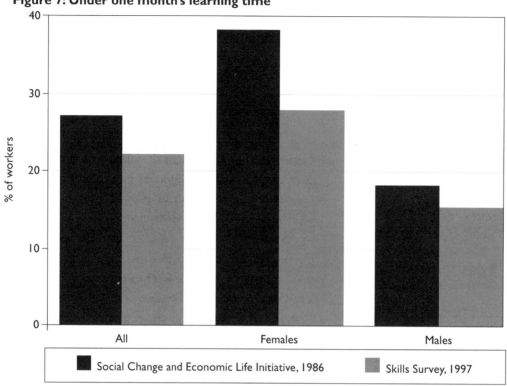

Source: Social Change and Economic Life Initiative, 1986; Skills Survey, 1997

Figure 8: Over two year's learning time

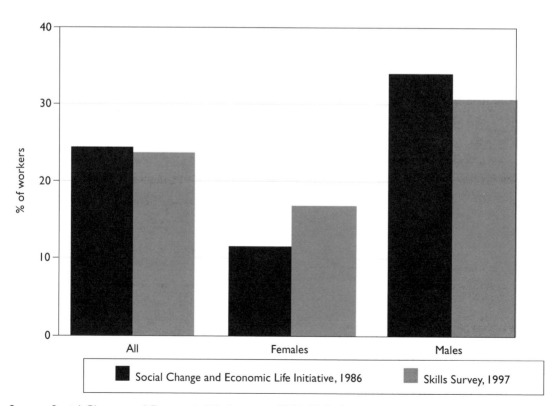

Source: Social Change and Economic Life Initiative, 1986; Skills Survey, 1997

Figure 9: Some qualifications required to get job

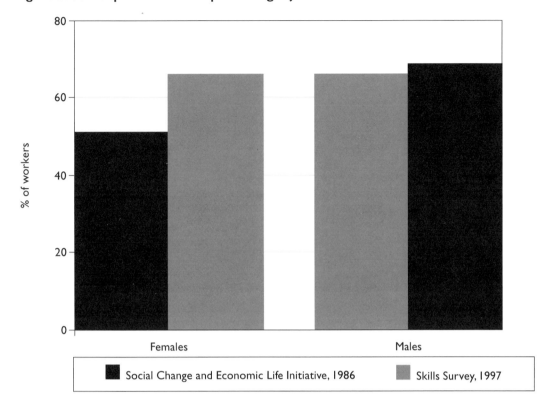

Source: Social Change and Economic Life Initiative, 1986; Skills Survey, 1997

Pattern by age

It might be hypothesised that the rapid expansion in the supply of well-educated young people entering employment over the last decade has been a – if not the – major factor in raising overall skill levels as recorded by various indicators. In other words, education may be enhancing the speed and abilities of workers to master and carry out their jobs rather than the jobs themselves becoming more demanding. To test this hypothesis we split the sample according to respondents' age: those under 35 years old we denote as 'young', those 35 years or over we refer to as 'old'. We examine whether the skills of the younger group have increased more than those comprising the older group. Each skill dimension is considered. Contrary to the hypothesis, the data show that older workers claim that their skill levels have risen faster than their younger counterparts. For example, among older workers the proportions needing only a short time to learn their jobs fell from 29% in 1986 to 21% in 1997, while for younger workers it fell less dramatically, from 25% to 22% (see Figure 10). It is therefore difficult on this evidence to sustain the argument that increased supply of qualifications among the young is driving skills upward.

Figure 10: Under one month's learning time

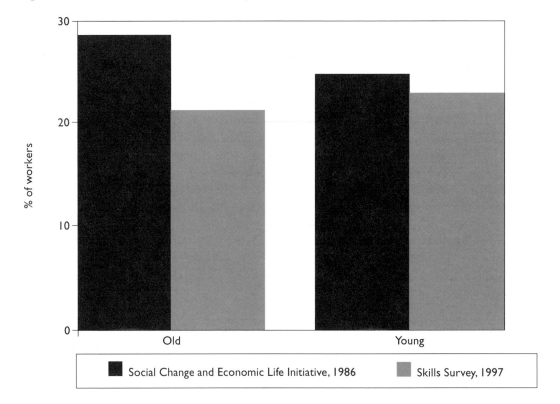

Source: Social Change and Economic Life Initiative, 1986; Skills Survey, 1997

Pattern by occupation

'Skills levels' are central to the Standard Occupational Classification (SOC) system. The classification is based either on the level of formal qualifications required for a person to get a particular job or on the duration of training and/or work experience normally required for occupational competence (OPCS, 1990, p 3; Elias, 1995, pp 43-5). It therefore makes sense to examine how the profile of Britain's employed workforce has changed over the period according to SOC. The 'top three' SOCs (which include occupations such as managers, teachers and scientists) have risen collectively in size by about six percentage points – rising from 29% of the workforce in 1986 to 35% in 1997. On the other, hand 'Craft' occupations (such as welders, electricians, metal workers, mechanics and tool makers) accounted for one in eight of workers in 1997 compared to one in six in 1986. This is consistent with the pattern of change shown in larger surveys such as the Labour Force Survey.

However, analysing skill trends by SOC alone is extremely hazardous since it fails to pick up changes within the various SOC categories (Kelleher et al, 1993). For example, the rising proportion of high level SOCs as recorded by our data need not necessarily indicate rising skill levels since these SOCs may now demand lower level skills than they did before. As it turns out, though, upskilling in these occupations is just as strong as recorded elsewhere. There is a statistically significant rise in skill for every occupation according to at least one measure. Thus, for 'Managers and Administrators' the skills increase is signalled by longer learning times, while for 'Plant and Machine Operators' it is highlighted by lengthier prior training.

Pattern by industry

The industrial spread of upskilling, however, is a little complex. While it is true that most industries exhibit a clear pattern of upskilling over the decade, notable exceptions remain. In the 'Wholesale and Retail' industry, for example, there is a statistically significant fall in the proportion of workers in jobs that take over two years to learn, while other indicators for this industry show only small and insignificant skill movements. Skill indicators in the 'Health and Social Work' industry provide a mixed picture. Jobs requiring short training periods have declined significantly, while at the same time those requiring lengthy learning times have been significantly reduced. On other measures little movement can be detected. If globalisation is one of the factors driving the pattern of upskilling our data identify, then one would expect the internationally exposed sectors of the economy to benefit most from the process of upskilling, while the insulated sectors would benefit least of all. This may provide part of the explanation for this pattern of skill change since neither the 'Whole and Retail' nor the 'Health and Social Work' industries are directly exposed to international competition. However, other industries – such as 'Education' – which are also protected from international competition, have experienced significant and strong skill increases. This suggests that the trajectory of skills in 'Wholesale and Retail' and 'Health and Social Work' may be anomalous. If so, they will need to be explained by more detailed industry analysis which takes into account specific industrial characteristics such as the introduction of GP fundholders and the formation of trust hospitals within the NHS.

Conclusion

Increased policy emphasis has recently been given to learning and skills. However, despite burgeoning interest in the subject, empirical data remains thin on the ground, and largely confined to the measurement of education participation rates and qualification attainment. The aim of this chapter has been to report on some of the results emerging from a comparison of data from two ESRC-supported surveys – the Skills Survey carried out in 1997 and the Social Change and Economic Life Initiative carried out in 1986.

The data suggest that upskilling has occurred since 1986 as measured in various ways. The employed British workforce is now more qualified than it was in 1986. More significantly, the results suggest that the jobs people do have changed. On average,

better qualifications are now required to get jobs and carry them out. In addition, jobs take longer to train for and take longer to learn to do well. Upskilling has affected young and old alike and all occupations have been upskilled in one way or another. Most industries appear to have benefited from rising skill levels. Women, however, have benefited more than men. The gap between women and men on all of the skill measures examined in this chapter has declined rapidly over time. However, the gender gap remains significant and pronounced according to most skill measures, but it has narrowed nonetheless.

The results of this analysis have a number of policy implications. First, it is noticeable that there appears to have been little overall change in the level of demand for degrees in Britain. Three out of 10 graduates in 1997 were in jobs for which a degree was not an entry requirement – a level similar to that recorded in 1986. This suggests a deficiency of employer demand and a cost to society in terms of underused (but paid for) human capital resources. The mismatch between the demand and supply of all qualifications is also alarmingly high – in 1997 around one in five of those holding any qualification reported that no qualification at all was required for the job they currently had. Secondly, our data provides little support for the hypothesis that the expansion of the education system over the last decade is driving upward overall skill levels. The data suggest that all age groups – and not just the young – experienced an upward movement in skills. This points, once again, to the importance of the demand-side in explaining patterns of skill change and by implication the means by which policy makers can influence the skills of the employed British workforce. Thirdly, exposure to international competition is sometimes considered to be the driving force behind upskilling with implications for trade policy. While here our results are preliminary, the analysis so far suggests that most sectors of the economy – both tradable and non-tradable – have experienced upskilling over the last decade. Trade policy would, therefore, appear to offer policy makers little leverage on the trajectory of skills. However, we intend to examine the linkage between international trade and skill movements in more detail in future work.

The Skills Survey also asked respondents about the importance of particular work tasks. This offers much more detailed insight into the tasks people perform at work. However, until another survey carries similar questions in future years, we have only limited information on how these particular work skills have changed over time (Green et al, 1999; Felstead et al, 1999). Just as we have compared the answers SCELI respondents gave to those given by SS respondents, we hope that future surveys of skills will be able to replicate some of the SS questions in order to provide academics and policy makers with more detail on how the skills of those in work are changing over time. Such a research agenda will complement evidence on the trajectory of change with finer grain detail on the type and nature of skills under focus, and will provide another round of policy implications for skills development and adjustment.

Notes

[1] This work has been financially supported by the Economic and Social Research Council (ESRC)'s 'Learning Society' Initiative directed by Frank Coffield (L123251032). For a more detailed discussion of these and other SS data see Green et al (1999).

[2] For this, the SS authors have collaborated with Dr Brendan Burchell.

[3] SS also gathered information on respondents' jobs five years ago; see Green et al (1999) and Felstead et al (1999).

[4] Ken Prandy of the University of Cambridge provided invaluable help and support which allowed us to recode the SCELI data in this way.

[5] The data in the text are rounded to the nearest whole number. However, the figures display the data rounded to the first decimal point.

[6] This is one type of credentialism. The other is when students increase their level of qualifications but not their understanding. We are grateful to Frank Coffield for pointing this out.

References

Ash, R.A. (1988) 'Job analysis in the world of work', in S. Gael (ed) *The job analysis handbook for business, industry and government*, vol 1, New York, NY: John Wiley.

Ashton, D. and Felstead, A. (1998) 'Organisational characteristics and skill formation in Britain: is there a link?', Paper presented to the *Work, Employment and Society* Conference, University of Cambridge, 14-16 September.

Ashton, D. and Green, F. (1996) *Education, training and the global economy*, Cheltenham: Edward Elgar.

Ashton, D., Davies, B., Felstead, A. and Green, F. (1999) *Workskills in Britain*, Oxford: SKOPE.

Becker, G.S. (1964) *Human capital*, New York, NY: National Bureau of Economic Research.

Bradley, M., Knight, I. and Kelly, M. (1997) 'Collecting qualifications data in sample surveys – a review of the methods used in government surveys', Research Paper RS10, London: DfEE.

Braverman, H. (1974) *Labor and monopoly capital*, New York, NY: Monthly Review Press.

Coombes, M., Wymer, C., Charlton, M., Bailey, S., Stonehouse, A. and Openshaw, S. (1997) 'Review of travel-to-work areas and small area unemployment rates', *Labour Market Trends*, vol 105, no 1, January, pp 9-12.

CSO (Central Statistical Office) (1993) *Standard Industrial Classification of economic activities: Correlation between SIC(92) and SIC(80)*, London: HMSO.

DfEE (Department for Education and Employment) (1996a) *Competitiveness and skills*, London: DfEE.

DfEE (1996b) *Education statistics 1996*, London: HMSO.

DfEE (1998) *The Learning Age: A renaissance for a new Britain*, London: HMSO.

DfEE and Cabinet Office (1996) *The Skills Audit: A report from an interdepartmental group*, London: DfEE and Cabinet Office.

Elias, P. (1995) 'Social class and the Standard Occupational Classification', in D. Rose (ed) *A report on Phase I of the ESRC review of the OPCS Social Classifications*, Swindon: ESRC.

European Commission (1994) *Growth, competitiveness and employment: The challenges and ways forward into the 21st century*, Luxembourg: Office of Official Publications of the European Communities.

Felstead, A. (1994) 'Funding government training schemes: mechanisms and consequences', *British Journal of Education and Work*, vol 7, no 3, September, pp 21-42.

Felstead, A. (1996) 'Identifying gender inequalities in the distribution of vocational qualifications in the UK', *Gender, Work and Organization*, vol 3, no 1, January, 1996, pp 38-50.

Felstead, A. (1997) 'Unequal shares for women? Qualification gaps in the National Targets for Education and Training', in H. Metcalf (ed) *Half our future: Women, skill development and training*, London: Policy Studies Institute.

Felstead, A. (1998) *Output-related funding in vocational education and training*, Luxembourg: Office of Official Publications of the European Communities.

Felstead, A., Ashton, D. and Green, F. (1999) *Justice for all? The pattern of skills in Britain*, University of Leicester Centre for Labour Market Studies, Working Paper No 23.

Financial Times (1993) 'Two-thirds of workforce show improved skill level', 7 June.

Gallie, D. (1991) 'Patterns of skill change: upskilling, deskilling or the polarization of skills?', *Work, Employment and Society*, vol 5, no 3, September, pp 319-51.

Gallie, D. (1994) 'Methodological appendix: the Social Change and Economic Life Initiative', in J. Rubery and F. Wilkinson (eds) *Employer strategy and the labour market*, Oxford: Oxford University Press.

Gallie, D. (1996) 'Skill, gender and the quality of employment', in R. Crompton, D. Gallie and K. Purcell (eds) *Changing forms of employment: Organisations, skills and gender*, London: Routledge.

Gallie, D. and White, M. (1993) *Employee commitment and the skills revolution*, London: Policy Studies Institute.

Green, A. and Steedman, H. (1997) 'Into the twenty first century: an assessment of British skill profiles and prospects', Centre for Economic Performance, London School of Economics and Political Science, mimeo.

Green, F. (1998) 'The value of skills', Paper presented to the EEEG Annual Conference, University of Newcastle, 29 June-1 July 1998.

Green, F., Ashton, D., Burchell, B., Davies, B. and Felstead, A. (1999) 'Are British workers getting more skilled?', in L. Borghans and A. de Grip (eds) *The over-educated worker? The economics of skill utilization*, Cheltenham: Edward Elgar.

ILO (International Labour Organisation) (1998) *World Employment Report, 1998*, Geneva: ILO.

Keep, E. and Mayhew, K. (1996) 'Evaluating the assumptions that underlie training policy', in A. Booth and D. Snower (eds) *Acquiring skills: Market failures, their symptoms and policy responses*, Cambridge: Cambridge University Press.

Kelleher, M., Scott, P. and Jones, B. (1993) 'Resistant to change? Some unexplained omissions in the 1990 Standard Occupational Classification', *Work, Employment and Society*, vol 7, no 3, September, pp 437-49.

Lloyd, C. (1997) 'Microelectronics in the clothing industry: firm strategy and the skills debate', *New Technology, Work and Employment*, vol 12, no 1, March, pp 36-47.

Marsh, C. and Vogler, C. (1994) 'Economic convergence: a tale of six cities', in D. Gallie, C. Marsh and C. Vogler (eds) *Social change and the experience of unemployment*, Oxford: Oxford University Press.

NACETT (National Advisory Council for Education and Training Targets) (1997) *Skills for 2000: Report on progress towards the National Targets for Education and Training*, London: NACETT.

OPCS (1990) *Standard Occupational Classification, Volume 1*, London: HMSO.

OPCS (1995) *LFS user's guide – Volume 5*, London: OPCS.

Pearsall, J. (ed) (1998) *The New Oxford Dictionary of English*, Oxford: Oxford University Press.

Prais, S. (1993) 'Economic performance and education: the nature of Britain's deficiencies', *National Institute of Economic and Social Research*, Discussion Paper No 52.

Primoff, E.S. and Fine, S.A. (1988) 'A history of job analysis', in S. Gael (ed) *The job analysis handbook for business, industry and government*, vol 1, New York, NY: John Wiley.

Robinson, P. and Manacorda, M. (1997) 'Qualifications and the labour market in Britain: 1984-94 skill biased change in the demand for labour or credentialism?', Centre for Economic Performance, London School of Economics and Political Science, Discussion Paper No 330, February.

Sloane, P., Battu, H. and Seaman, P. (1995) 'Over-education, under-education and the British labour market', University of Aberdeen Working Paper 95-09.

Steedman, H. (1997) 'The Skills Audit: who's winning the race?', *CentrePiece*, vol 2, issue 1, February, pp 10-13.

Steedman, H., Mason, G. and Wagner, K. (1991) 'Intermediate skills in the workplace: deployment, standards and supply in Britain, France and Germany', *National Institute of Economic Review*, no 136, May.

Stevens, M. (1994) 'A theoretical model of on-the-job training with imperfect competition', *Oxford Economic Papers*, vol 46, no 4, pp 537-62.

Turok, I. (1997) 'Should travel-to-work areas be replaced?', *Working Brief*, issue 82, March, pp 17-18.

Webster, D. (1997) 'Travel-to-work areas (TTWAs) and local unemployment statistics: a Glasgow view', Paper presented to *The Future of TTWAs – Alternative Approaches to Defining Local Labour Markets for Urban and Regional Policy* Conference, Rosebery House, Edinburgh, 29 January.

Appendix

The relevant skills questions drawn upon in this chapter are:

- Which qualifications do you have, starting with the highest qualifications? [Identical response sets were used in the two surveys. However, the SCELI data were collected as an element of the work history section of the survey. Respondents were first asked whether they had gained any qualifications by the age of 14, and then asked about those gained at any time subsequently.]

- If they were applying today, what qualifications, if any, would someone need to get the type of job you have now?

- How necessary do you think it is to possess those qualifications to do your job competently?

- How long did it take for you after you first started doing this type of job to learn to do it well? [If answers 'still learning' ask: How long do you think it will take?]

- Since completing full-time education, have you ever had, or are you currently undertaking, training for the type of work that you currently do? [If 'yes', How long, in total, did (or will) that training last?]

6

Adult guidance services for a learning society? Evidence from England

Will Bartlett and Teresa Rees

Introduction

The economic recovery which took place in the UK in the mid-to-late 1990s has given rise to an increasing awareness that sustainable economic growth depends upon the development of high technology and information-based industries which require an increasingly highly skilled workforce. Some commentators and policy makers (DfEE, 1998) have argued that the period of sustained growth, which has been even more pronounced in the USA, already reflects this transition to an information-based economy and a learning society which holds the potential to eliminate or at least reduce the worst effects of the business cycle. At the same time labour markets have had to adapt to the twin pressures of globalisation and technological change. This has come about in the UK and the USA, but to a lesser extent in mainland European economies through an increased use of fixed-term and/or part-time labour contracts. In these economies labour market participants are expected to make frequent job changes in the course of their working lives.

In the UK the government has actively promoted the deregulation of the labour market, reducing the employment protection previously granted to the workforce. Companies have 'downsized' and 'delayered', reducing their core of permanent workers and increasing their employment of part-timers and contract workers. Flexible employment contracts are the order of the day resulting in the "death of career" (Collin and Watts, 1996) and a dramatic reshaping of the employment relationship. Watts has referred to this process as the

"Careerquake" (Watts, 1996a). Although the average length of job tenure has not decreased (Burgess and Rees, 1997), changes from one job to another increasingly involve transitions between job types, and between employment and retraining, rather than simple lay-off and re-hire into the same place of employment, or even into the same industry or occupation. In this context, transition between jobs in the flexible labour market is intrinsically connected with periodic entry and re-entry into spells of education and training. As mobility between flexible jobs becomes a more central component of post-Fordist society, in contrast to the traditional progression up a hierarchical career ladder, so the importance of adult careers guidance is increasing. This, together with the rapid expansion of adult education opportunities in the UK in recent years, highlights the important role of adult educational guidance, in combination with the adult vocational guidance required by increasing labour market flexibility.

Historically, in the UK, the vocational and educational guidance systems have evolved along rather different routes. Vocational guidance has been situated mainly in the Careers Services which were established following the 1973 Employment and Training Act and were run by local authorities. Their principal focus has been on provision of guidance for school leavers, although in some cases they have also provided limited services to adults, especially after the abolition of the Occupation Guidance Service in 1981. Educational guidance has been provided as an integrated service within schools, colleges and universities. Educational guidance for adults outside the education system has remained limited, although in some localities Educational Guidance Services for Adults (EGSAs) have been established following the innovative experience of the Belfast EGSA which was established as a voluntary organisation in 1967. In this paper and in other publications arising from this research project we refer to both vocational and educational guidance services as 'career guidance services'. This terminology highlights the breakdown of traditional hierarchical career progression, and the increasing need for individuals to take responsibility for, and to manage their lifetime 'career' which may involve multiple individual 'careers', and both vertical and horizontal transitions – vertical, in the sense of a linear progression to successively higher levels of responsibility within an industry, and horizontal, in the sense of transition between industries and occupational levels.

The new developments in the labour market and in the organisation of work and 'career' lie at the root of the call for the development of a learning society. As argued by Watts (1997), a new approach to learning and work is beginning to develop which includes both formal and non-formal aspects of career. This new approach encompasses non-formal approaches to learning in the workplace. The proposed University for Industry is one example of the potential of this approach. Non-formal work also includes unpaid but socially valuable work in households and the community. This wide conception of the notion of career opens up new possibilities for participation and for social inclusion in a learning society. In another paper (Rees and Bartlett, 1999) we have identified three distinct models of the Learning Society. The first is the 'skill growth' model which emphasises the link between skill formation and economic growth. In this view, career guidance is instrumental and deterministic, providing a brokerage service for individuals in search of particular jobs or training courses.

The second is the 'personal development' model, which is more concerned with facilitating individual self-fulfilment by provision of resources to enable individuals to make informed choices about their preferred modes of participation in learning and work. This model links more closely to the new view of career outlined above, and

implies a more client-centred and voluntaristic role for the guidance services.

The third model we have called the 'social learning' model which emphasises the embeddedness of the learning process in the social and community context in which individuals are situated. This model implies a more action-orientated role for guidance services in which guidance providers work alongside individuals rather than acting as independent experts. Examples can be found in the Italian experience with social cooperatives in which disadvantaged individuals work alongside guidance workers in a cooperative enterprise. Clearly, these different conceptions of a learning society imply radically different approaches to policy. However, in all three cases, there is a growing consensus of the importance of career guidance for adults as an active and central element in its development, a view shared by the National Advisory Group for Continuing Education and Lifelong Learning which argues that "the provision of up-to-date, accessible and impartial information and advice will be essential if a strategy of lifelong learning for all is to be successful" (Fryer, 1997).

The key question, therefore, is to identify ways in which such objectives can be achieved. In the UK, under the Conservative government, enormous changes took place in the way the State is involved in supporting and dealing with the consequences of economic growth and structural change through its provision of welfare programmes. Further radical changes can be expected to emerge during the tenure of the current Labour government, of which the New Deal programme to facilitate job search and job entry of young and long-term unemployed individuals is but one relevant example. During the 1990s the welfare state has been transformed through the introduction of new arrangements designed to emulate market processes in the provision of public services in many areas, including health, education and community care (Le Grand and Bartlett, 1993; Bartlett et al, 1998). One of the latest areas to experience this process of marketisation has been the Careers Service, which was contracted out by competitive tender to a range of independent providers, some of which are conversions of the previous local authority services and others which are completely new entrants into the field. Moreover, other agencies such as TECs also became progressively more involved in the career guidance field, and the delivery systems which they developed bear some of the hallmarks of a quasi-market. We have discussed some of the implications of this process elsewhere (Bartlett, 1996; Bartlett and Rees, 1997; see also Watts, 1998), but this paper is the first in which we have been able to draw upon the results of a series of in-depth case studies of the effects of these changes on guidance systems in England carried out as part of an ESRC project.

The purpose of the paper is to outline the recent developments in the adult career guidance system in England on the basis of empirical evidence gathered from a set of linked case studies of four separate localities. In the next section we outline the basic structure of the adult guidance services in the UK, and in the third section we summarise the comparative features of the adult guidance systems in each of the four localities in the study. In the fourth section we discuss some of the key issues in relation to the adult guidance system which we have investigated in the project on the basis of the case study evidence, and the final section provides a conclusion.

The structure of the adult guidance system in the UK

The Careers Services and the Training and Enterprise Councils

Traditionally the vocational guidance service in the UK has been based around the local Careers Services run and managed by Local Education Authorities (LEAs) (Killeen and Kidd, 1996). Their statutory responsibility has been to provide guidance to school pupils, school leavers, students in vocational part-time education, people under the age of 19 not in education or training, and people with special educational needs of any age to assist them in their choice of career. In a few areas the Careers Services had established adult guidance services funded and promoted by the local authorities who saw the emerging need. However, the main stimulus to the development of adult guidance services came from the employer-led Training and Enterprise Councils (TECs) established in England and Wales in the late 1980s

(Hawthorn, 1996a). These organisations were responsible for implementing the government's vocational training programmes for employees, the unemployed and youth training on a decentralised locality basis, and in doing so were drawn into the provision of adult guidance services. The TECs are typically funded by bidding for resources from various government programmes, normally channelled through the regional Government Office. These programmes have recently been gathered together in the Single Regeneration Budget (SRB) and so TECs are often competing for funds from this source, augmented by matched funding in many cases from the European Social Fund (ESF).

In other cases TECs bid directly to government departments for specific programme funds. In the case of adult guidance two particularly important sources of funding (at least up until 1996) have been the Gateways programme (for unemployed adults) and the Skill Choice programme (for employed adults). The TECs themselves would typically contract out adult guidance services to a range of providers within their locality who would be in competition with one another for TEC funds. In this way a quasi-market in adult guidance was established, based on a separation of the purchase and the provision of services. In a few experimental cases, the purchasing function in these quasi-markets was devolved to the users of the services through voucher schemes (for example, under the Gateways programme). But mainly the quasi-market was structured through a competitive contracting out to service providers who would be funded either on a block contract or a capitation basis.

Under the 1993 Trade Union Reform and Employment Rights Act a fundamental change in the way careers services were organised and funded took place. As in other areas of public service, such as health, education and community care, there was an attempt to introduce market-type forces (quasi-markets) into the provision of the service. In the case of the careers service this was to be achieved through a competition for the right to supply services in a particular locality (contracting out). Careers Services were privatised and removed from LEA control, and funded on the basis of a contract specified directly with the State (the Department for Education and Employment through the regional Government Offices). The new providers retained a statutory duty to provide guidance services to school pupils as before and these services were provided free of charge at the point of delivery, paid for by the State through the contract. The core contract which covered 85% of the budget was funded by a capitation formula based on the number of school pupils in an area, augmented by a target-based element of funding covering the remaining 15% which was linked to the number of action plans achieved with the client group. A system of competitive tendering for guidance contracts on an area basis was introduced. By 1997 all the LEA Careers Services had been converted to private companies or partnerships and contracted out. Most were converted into partnerships of LEAs and TECs, and Local Enterprise Companies (LECs) in Scotland. In a few cases, however, entirely new service providers have entered the field and the Careers Service retained a separate identity from the TEC. Nearly all the new careers companies were set up as companies limited by guarantee, often with a non-profit status, although some were established as companies limited by shares and other legal forms (Chatrik, 1997).

Where the new careers companies were organised as LEA/TEC partnerships, the two main organisations providing adult guidance were brought together. In these cases often the TEC provides direct block funding to the careers company to support the provision of adult guidance services by the company. In effect the competitive quasi-market in provision of services by TEC-funded providers is replaced by the prior competition for the contract to deliver the careers service. In cases where the careers service contract was won by an independent company, this fusion did not take place, and the TEC continued to act as an independent purchaser of adult guidance services on the local quasi-market. These two models of provision which have emerged since the implementation of the 1993 Act are clearly visible in the locality case studies reported below.

The Employment Service

The Employment Service is an Executive Agency of the State (Department for Education and Employment) which is responsible for administering the Jobseekers' Allowance, providing information about vacancies to unemployed jobseekers, and providing a recruitment service to employers. Their primary function is job placement, and each office is set targets for job placement rates to be achieved. There are additional targets based on certain categories, for example, for disabled people, and the long-term unemployed. Funding is provided through a core contract augmented by a variable amount related to achievement of targets.

The Employment Service provides a limited range of guidance services. However, these are mainly oriented towards achieving the job placement targets, rather than providing guidance in the more general sense of promoting individual career development. The first intervention takes place when an unemployed person has failed to find work within a period of 13 weeks. It consists of a programme called 'Job Search Plus' designed to provide help with training on CV writing and other job search skills. This training is externally contracted to private organisations or to the local TEC, giving a further example of quasi-market provision of adult guidance. After six months unemployment, claimants go into the 'Job Finder' programme, which involves interviews with Employment Service advisors. This is a relatively new programme started early in 1997, and provides a series of interviews once a fortnight over a 14-week period. After 12 months of unemployment there is a further externally contracted provision called 'Job Plan', which gives a one-week course, followed up by interviews with advisors to consolidate it. After two years unemployment claimants go on Restart programme which involves more courses.

One of the main routes through which the Employment Service delivers adult guidance services is through a further scheme known as the 'Job Club' which is available to claimants who remain unemployed for over six months. The Job Club services are contracted to external providers including private companies, colleges, charities, and in some cases to the Careers Service. The Job Club and other programmes give training in job search skills, but do not provide educational guidance. They are also specialised in the provision of labour market information. The Job Club runs formal sessions on interview techniques and CVs, and employers are brought in to talk about their business. The Job Club leader should have sufficient knowledge of the local labour market opportunities available so that they can provide guidance services to clients. The training of Job Club leaders used to be provided in-house, but now it is contracted out. All programmes include access to the 'Adult Directions' skills evaluation computer programme and in some cases group leaders will refer people to local adult guidance providers.

In contrast to the Careers Service and the TECs, local Employment Service offices have little local autonomy. External contracting is bound by Treasury guidelines. There is typically a regional list of preferred providers who are invited to tender for particular contracts for externally provided services and who are selected on criteria of value for money. A tender evaluation and scoring system is used to select and monitor the successful providers.

Concern over the persistence of long-term unemployment has led to the introduction of a number of new innovative programmes to create jobs for the long-term unemployed. 'Project Work' was an innovative approach to Welfare to Work introduced by the Conservative government which gave long-term unemployed claimants 13 weeks intensive help by the Employment Service. Claimants who had no success in getting a job were referred to an external provider for job experience placement. Pilot projects were carried out in Humberside and Maidstone and were very successful. Since that time the new Labour government has come into power with its own approach in a scheme called 'New Deal'. The emphasis of this new programme is on 16- to 25-year-olds as well as the long-term unemployed. A key element of the scheme is on placing 18- to 24-year-olds who have been out of work for six months with employers who receive a £60 per week subsidy, backed up by training through one day a week release to study for NVQ together with options for full-time education. It is expected that about 250,000 young people could be involved. Help will also be given to over-25s unemployed for over two years who will be eligible for a similar subsidy programme, with six months training. Employers will be closely involved in this scheme through a new partnership approach. It is possible that this programme may lead to closer links between the Employment Service and the Careers Service, and several of the respondents of this study from the Employment Service favoured the

integration of the Careers Service into the Employment Service.

The private and voluntary sectors

It is often claimed that there is limited scope for the provision of guidance services on the private market (Watts, 1996b; our interviewees). Nevertheless there is a thriving private market in some areas of provision of adult guidance. The private sector has operated successfully in two main areas. Firstly, in the provision of outplacement and redundancy services for companies undergoing restructuring, and secondly, through the work of recruitment agencies, which have an increasingly important role in brokering job placements in the flexible, part-time and temporary contract labour markets. While the former group of private providers offer services in the mainstream of guidance counselling (skills assessment, psychometric testing, job search skills training), the latter are more placement driven, and offer only a peripheral range of guidance services as such, although they are increasingly being drawn into government-funded training programmes in collaboration with the TECs. The key point to note about both these sectors, however, is that the main source of funding is almost invariably through charges and fees on employers (although recruitment agencies also make deductions from employees' wages).

Alongside the private sector a large number of guidance service providers have been established in the voluntary sector, often offering services to specific disadvantaged groups, particularly among ethnic minorities, but also more general adult guidance services. In many cases the growth of these voluntary sector providers has been stimulated by the quasi-market for guidance services organised and funded by the TECs. However, where the TEC-funded quasi-market has been replaced by a LEA/TEC partnership, and where this has led to a redirection of TEC funds directly to the Careers Service to fund adult guidance provision, the role of the voluntary sector may be expected to diminish.

Further and Higher Education

Another key provider of adult guidance services is the Further Education (FE) and Higher Education (HE) sectors. These sectors are quite distinct from one another in terms of the nature and range of services which they provide. The FE sector was taken out of local authority control by the 1992 Further and Higher Education Act. Funding is now channelled through the Further Education Funding Council (FEFC). Further Education colleges normally provide limited careers and education guidance, usually supplemented by services supplied by the Careers Service, which, under the 1973 Employment and Training Act, are required to offer guidance services to full-time students in FE colleges (Hawthorn, 1996b). The largest element of guidance in colleges is 'entry guidance' funded by the FEFC grant to colleges. However, this is geared towards promoting enrolment of individual students on college courses, and is sometimes criticised on the grounds that there is little incentive to provide unbiased advice to prospective students. Nevertheless, as one of our interviewees points out, this danger is modified by the fact that part of the FEFC funding is also linked to the course completion rates and so the impact of potential bias is probably less than is sometimes claimed.

The main problem with FE college guidance services is that they are severely limited in scope. Most colleges provide only a minimal service. In contrast university careers offices are well provided for, often with a substantial staff and a dedicated office or a separate building. Core funding typically comes from the university's own resources, but often there is also a substantial input from employers, especially the larger corporations. The case study material provides ample evidence of the relatively favoured position of the HE sector. A number of key issues for the HE sector have been identified in a recent report of the National Institute for Careers Education and Counselling (Watts, 1997). One of the most important concerns the possibility of extending the scope of the HE guidance services to groups outside the immediate clientele of the university sector. Watts identifies a number of possibilities including continuing lifelong provision of services to all university graduates, beyond graduation. One could also speculate whether it could be possible to open these university services to adult non-graduates, or to enhance the collaboration between the university sector and the adult guidance sector more generally. In other words, can town and gown collaborate in the provision of adult guidance services?

Other providers: the Probation Service and the Armed Forces

A range of other providers also operate to deliver guidance services to particular special needs groups. Prominent among these is the Probation Service which is beginning to offer careers and education guidance to ex-offenders. These initiatives are funded by the Home Office which is beginning to make a link between the lack of employment opportunities for ex-offenders and the incidence of re-offending. As a result, a number of new initiatives are being sponsored designed to promote the employability of ex-offenders and boost their employment prospects. A second main area outside the mainstream is the provision of guidance services to retiring members of the Armed Forces. This area of work is given greater prominence recently due to the end of the Cold War and the reaping of the peace dividend. The Armed Forces are downsizing in turn and retired military personal have unique problems in making the transition to civilian life which requires special assistance from guidance professionals. Hitherto, these have been provided by a branch of the Regular Forces Employment Association which receives 80% of its funding from the Ministry of Defence and 20% from various charities. The 'resettlement services' are run by the Tri-Service Resettlement organisation which provides a range of guidance services depending on length of service, including how to write CVs, briefing on different industries, and in-depth guidance interviews. Retiring personnel also receive a grant of £500 to do any 28-day course they want to top up their skills, for example, HGV driving, or a business course. The whole of the Tri-Service Resettlement organisation is being privatised and will in future be managed by Coutts Career Consultants, which won the competition between 160 companies that bid for the right to run the service.

Adult guidance in four localities

Four English localities were selected as the case studies for this project on the basis of two main criteria: (a) the type of careers company which had been established and (b) the degree of tightness in the local labour market. The first criterion was designed to capture differences between careers companies by legal form. Two of the case studies were chosen to represent cases where incumbents had been converted into LEA/TEC partnerships, and two to represent cases of new entry by newly established careers companies. The second criterion was designed to provide variation in the labour market environment in terms of the level of unemployment. In addition a further locality in Scotland, Fife, was included to capture the Scottish dimension of guidance services, although in this paper we focus on the case of England alone.

Table 1: Case study areas according to selection criteria

	LEA/TEC partnership	New entrant career companies
Low unemployment	Area A	Area D
High unemployment	Area B	Area C

In this section we highlight a few key comparative features of the guidance system which have emerged from this study, before going on in the next section to identify key issues for debate. The four localities reveal the diversity in patterns of provision which have emerged.

Area A: LEA/TEC partnership – low unemployment

This is a prosperous area in the South West of England with low unemployment. The Careers Service is provided by a LEA/TEC partnership set up in 1993 as a non-profit company limited by guarantee. It provides adult guidance through its specialised consultancy division. This division provides redundancy counselling services to companies and to private clients who are charged between £45 and £170 for individual guidance services. From this activity, the company earns a surplus which supports the free adult guidance services provided by its main division, which is also supported financially by the TEC. The careers company has established a city centre guidance 'shop' which serves 26,000 'customers' per year, half of whom are adults. The shop provides a basic information service to 80% of its customers and

interviews to about 20%. The company has extensive links with employers and visits are made to over 1,000 employers each year to canvass for vacancies and advertise their services. Another division of the company delivers the TEC lifelong learning programme through various adult education projects in collaboration with employers, colleges and local community groups. The company has service level agreements with local colleges to provide careers counselling to college students on site, although this is limited to the statutory age groups. In contrast to the limited guidance offered to adult students at the colleges, the university has a well resourced careers office, which is supported by significant inputs from large national businesses. Area A also has a thriving private guidance sector. This is financed by charging fees to companies for redundancy and outplacement counselling. Typically, companies are charged between £500 and £5,000 per employee for these services. Recruitment agencies are also active in the local labour market and one such agency interviewed in the project is a training provider for the TEC. Although recruits are sometimes referred to the careers service for guidance the agency also provides in-house guidance to its clients.

Area B: LEA/TEC partnership – high unemployment

This area is an old industrial city in the north of England with high levels of unemployment. The careers company is a LEA/TEC partnership, as in Area A. It is limited by guarantee but is also registered as a charity. The company has a specialised adult guidance division, which is virtually a monopoly provider of adult guidance services in the city. It is supported mainly by funding directly from the TEC and the ESF, but also from a variety of other sources of funding including contracts from the Employment Service and the regional SRB. There has been a noticeable increase in the amount of adult guidance work provided since the company became independent. The company has a city centre careers library which is used by 50,000 people per year. Guidance interviews are provided on a means-tested basis, with charges for those who are required to pay ranging from £35 to almost £100 for various types of service, and in all provide about 3,000 interviews per year. There is a close relationship between the Careers Service and the TEC which contracts out most of the adult guidance work to the Careers Service, and only a small part to other providers, including local colleges and universities. The TEC also provides its own education guidance service for adults, catering to about 4,500 people each year. This service is heavily used by the long-term unemployed who are referred to them by the Employment Service. A distinguishing feature of the adult guidance system in Area B is the strong element of collaboration and networking between the various agencies involved.

Area C: New entrant careers company – high unemployment

The two boroughs in Area C have some of the highest unemployment rates in the UK (22% and 17% respectively). They are served by a careers company which is part of a large regional conglomerate, comprising five separate careers services. The parent careers company is limited by shares, and has an overtly entrepreneurial outlook, with a focus on commercial as well as professional success. It has a complex ownership structure. The shareholders include the parent careers company, a county council, colleges, employers and staff, as well as another private company specialising in providing support for small and medium-sized enterprise development in the UK and internationally whose shareholders in turn include a county council, some major financial institutions and a range of individuals. The parent company claims to be one of the largest of the new careers companies in the UK, and believes that its size provides it with significant economies of scale. The impression gained from the project field work is that the Careers Service is not a major provider of adult guidance services. There is no careers guidance shop and the main offices of the Careers Service are located in premises which are inconspicuous and moreover are shared with the local Employment Service. In the same building there is a residual adult education service funded by the local council, which has struggled to maintain its independence from the Careers Service. However, despite this, the proximity to the Employment Service appears to deter unemployed claimants from seeking advice due to anxieties about loss of benefits.

The main source of funding for adult guidance comes from the local TEC. Being a separate entity from the Careers Service, the TEC is not tied to purchasing guidance services from the Careers Service. Instead it contracts out the guidance work to a wide range of local providers, including the Careers Service, but also a large number of organisations in the voluntary sector based around specific community groups, charities, colleges as well as a network of private guidance providers. These providers of adult guidance are funded through block contracts let on a competitive basis by the TEC and provide a mix of free services and means tested fee-charged services to around 3,000 clients per year. The contracts specify targets, which include targets for increasing the numbers of fee-charged services provided. Although the extent of adult guidance provision funded by the TEC appears low, the TEC also runs its own telephone helpline with a budget of £40,000 which reaches out to a wider client group. In the opinion of the TEC respondent the "problem with the [adult] guidance sector [in the borough] is that it is so fragmented". Reflecting the low level of provision of adult guidance services in the boroughs, the local colleges attempt to fill a gap. For example, the local community college provides a wide range of guidance services, based on funding from a variety of sources including the Employment Service (which funds a job search unit), the local borough (which funds a unit for truants), the local health authority (for mental patients), the National Association for the Care and Resettlement of Offenders (NACRO) (for ex-offenders) and so on. The college also has three part-time community development workers who provide services through local community groups. As in other localities the local university also has a well-resourced careers office, although this is relatively underfunded compared to the more established universities in Areas A and B, and relies to a great extent on an internal networked computer information system to provide information about job opportunities to its students.

Area D: New entrant careers company – low unemployment

This area is based around a prosperous 'boom town' in the south of England with low unemployment

(2% in 1997) and one of the highest levels of GDP per capita in the country. The careers company is a branch of a large independent company specialising in the provision of education courses teaching English as a foreign language, and school inspections. Unlike most other careers company organisations, it is a global company with 4,000 employees worldwide and a turnover of £30m. The company is limited by guarantee and has charitable status. It won the contract to provide careers services in 1995, and has also expanded to provide the careers service in a number of other areas. The careers service division is the fastest expanding part of the company, with a turnover of £11m. As with the careers company in Area C, the company believes there are significant economies of scale to be achieved in the provision of guidance services.

However, this belief does not extend to the provision of adult guidance and the company has decided not to establish an adult guidance unit as "the market is too limited to provide a worthwhile commercial prospect", according to the company's chief executive. Consequently it has fallen to the local TEC to provide adult guidance services which it does by contracting out services to local providers, mainly in the voluntary sector. However, the various TEC initiatives in this field have been unsuccessful in generating funds from government programmes, employers or the Employment Service. A limited residual service including a 'Skill Bus' and a telephone helpline have been established funded mainly by the ESF. In addition reserves built up from the Training for Work programme are used to finance adult guidance services through a number of voluntary sector providers and from local FE colleges. In the light of this experience, the view of the TEC is that the greatest unmet need in conditions of a tight labour market is for adult guidance services for employees in work to enable job-to-job transitions which can underpin flexibility in the labour market. "If the objective of a learning society is to develop skills, you don't do it by focusing resources on marginal groups such as the unemployed" (TEC respondent). In these circumstances, the main activities in the field of adult guidance in Area D are carried out by small voluntary groups catering for severely disadvantaged groups in the labour market. One such group, based at the local FE college, provides services to long-term unemployed, women returners to work,

disabled adults, ethnic minorities and ex-offenders. However, such services are small-scale and face budget cuts. The only disadvantaged group with a relatively secure level of provision is ex-offenders who benefit from an innovative project based at the local Probation Service. In contrast the local university has a large careers office and is well resourced with strong financial and in-kind backing from employers who stand to benefit from a well-informed pool of graduate labour.

Overall, the four localities included in the case study display noticeable differences in the structure of provision of adult guidance services. Broadly, adult guidance services appear to be better developed in Areas A and B than in Areas C and D. These differences appear to be connected more with the organisational form of the guidance services than with the state of the local labour markets, that is, the differences reflect different provider orientations rather than the needs of the local population.

Comparisons

While both Areas B and C suffer high levels of unemployment, Area B has a more developed adult guidance provision based upon a commitment of the local TEC to fund services out of its reserves, the existence of a dedicated adult guidance division of the Careers Service, and a well-organised collaborative network of providers. In Area C, although the local TEC has a commitment to adult guidance, it does not work in close collaboration with the careers company and provision is fragmented among a plethora of voluntary and community groups. Local colleges work hard to plug the gaps but their primary focus is on attracting students onto courses rather than the provision of independent advice. Moreover, they struggle to attract funding from a diverse set of funding bodies.

In contrast, the other two localities, Areas A and D, both enjoy high levels of economic activity and low unemployment. Nevertheless they too differ in the extent of provision of adult guidance services. In Area A, the local Careers Service has a dedicated section providing adult guidance on a consultancy basis to companies and also to a more limited extent to individuals. There is a city centre guidance shop providing highly visible services to the public with a high proportion of adults among the users of the service. There is close collaboration with the local TEC which has a strong commitment to the provision of guidance services to adults. In addition there is a thriving private sector, which attracts a substantial amount of business from employers. By contrast, in Area D, which has similarly low unemployment, the provision of adult guidance is extremely limited. The careers company has withdrawn from the provision of adult guidance and views it as an unprofitable market. And the local TEC, although recognising the importance of adult guidance, both for employees and the marginalised unemployed, struggles to obtain funding and appears less willing to use its own reserves to finance adult guidance services than in Area A.

A key factor in determining the extent of provision therefore appears to be the way in which the Careers Services and the TECs interact in different cases. Where interaction is close and collaborative, the transition to a contracted-out Careers Service appears to have generated a dynamic and innovative approach to the expansion of guidance services for adults. This interaction appears to be best achieved in cases where there is a formal organisational partnership on which to base the work of the Careers Service and where the Careers Services and the TECs are fused together in a formal organisational structure based on the formation of careers companies as LEA/TEC partnerships. Elsewhere, in cases where such interaction is absent or made more difficult by the entry of independent careers companies without close links to the TEC structures, the provision of adult guidance is placed on a less coherent and more fragmented basis. In these cases the TEC appears to have a lesser interest and ability to stimulate the provision of adult guidance services, and the Careers Services are more focused on the provision of commercially viable services to the statutory groups in schools and colleges. Moreover, TEC-funded contracted-out provision is fragmented and small-scale and fails to benefit from the economies of scale which the large independent careers companies identify as important in their statutory activity.

Conclusions

Provision of adult guidance

On a national level the provision of adult guidance is patchy. The quality and range of services offered to users depends very much on the accident of where one happens to live. Moreover, this spatial variation bears no relationship to need as expressed by differences in labour market conditions. At present, where adult guidance services are provided on a free or means-tested basis they are generally only provided to users living within the area covered by the service provider in question. An obvious solution to the problem of spatial differentiation would be to introduce a means of funding 'cross border' flows of users. This can probably only be done through a national funding formula, perhaps based on a system of vouchers, similar to that used by the Corporation of London in financing 'out-of-area' provision of training and education for its adult learners. The use of vouchers in the provision of adult guidance (through the Gateways and Skill Choice programmes) have so far been assessed as failures. But these were only local experiments. The new Learning Line telephone helpline will be a government-funded scheme linked to local guidance providers. However, unless backed up by funding for out-of-area referrals it may only tend to reinforce existing inequalities in the pattern of provision.

Funding

Funding for adult guidance depends upon the ability of careers companies to generate surpluses, and on the policy of the local TEC towards funding provision through Careers Services or networks of independent providers. It also depends on the ability of these organisations to access external contract funding from a wide variety of sources prominent among which are the ESF, the regional SRB, and to a lesser extent other government departments such as the Home Office (in the case of ex-offenders) and from charities. There is also substantial funding for education guidance in colleges funded through the FEFC, and for careers guidance for graduates through university careers offices, arguably an already privileged group of adults. Apart from this, adult guidance services depend upon the ability of individuals to pay individual fees for services, but the take-up of such services appears to be low. It is argued that there is only a limited market for adult guidance services, and yet there is a thriving private sector for redundancy counselling and for outplacement services. This private sector activity is funded substantially by employers, but on the whole it is only employees of the larger corporate employers who benefit. One possible solution to the funding gap would be though contributions from employers using a compulsory levy as in France (Rees et al, 1999) which underpins a system of 'skills assessments' for employed adults. Such a scheme could potentially also be funded through National Insurance. Government subsidies could be channelled through the proposed 'Learning Accounts' (DfEE, 1998). Alternatively, private insurance could be an option. Some schemes are beginning to emerge linking guidance provision into voluntary private unemployment and redundancy insurance provided by credit card companies as well as banks and insurance companies. These could be encouraged and extended.

Disadvantaged groups

The general fragmentation and patchiness of provision for adults are intensified in the provision of services for disadvantaged groups. Although many Careers Services and TECs are sensitive to the needs of disadvantaged groups including the long-term unemployed, women returners to work, ex-offenders and ethnic minority groups, there is a lack of strategic focus towards them. Guidance services for such groups often rely on the activity of voluntary and community groups which operate on a relatively small-scale. Colleges of Further Education are particularly active in this field, although often with a primary interest in attracting users to the courses on offer. Moreover, employer biases against certain categories of workers, for example, older workers, remain a structural problem which guidance services are ill-equipped to tackle. For younger adults suffering long-term unemployment the New Deal programme offers some hope of job placement. However, unless this has an effective guidance element, it is possible that it will suffer the defects of previous youth-oriented programmes in being more a means of reducing government unemployment statistics than a benefit to the young people in need that it is supposed to

help. Indeed, a recent report indicates that as many as one quarter of the 8,200 people who joined the New Deal programme in its pilot stage in January 1998 had dropped out, and that many of the jobs offered fail to provide adequate training opportunities (*Sunday Times*, 2 August 1998).

The effect of the privatisation of the Careers Service on adult guidance provision

The most radical policy initiative in the area of guidance services in recent years was carried through by the Conservative government when in 1993 it began to contract out the provision of guidance services to a set of new careers companies. In the majority of cases these were LEA/TEC partnerships which essentially represented conversions of the existing Careers Services into new independent companies with a substantial involvement of the local TEC. In a few cases entirely new entrants into the sector won the contract competition. This research project has shown that there is some evidence that there has been a substantially different outcome with regard to the provision of adult guidance services depending on the type of companies which won the contracts. The main finding has been that LEA/TEC partnerships have been more effective at providing adult guidance than the new entrants which have concentrated on the provision of core services to the statutory client groups. They have done so not only for commercial reasons, but also because of a lack of integration of services with the TECs. Does this mean that the entry of new providers or the expansion of the 'independents' should be discouraged? We do not think that this is a necessary implication. The new entrants appear to able to provide a cost-effective service, and by expanding appear to gain economies of scale. If further contracting competitions are to be carried out in the future it is possible that the more dynamic companies will expand into new areas and that ultimately guidance services in England will be delivered by a handful of the more aggressive and cost-effective providers. This would be a beneficial outcome in some respects although the provision of adult guidance services would be likely to suffer. The new Labour government has indicated that there will be a shift away from contracting to licensing, so that in future contracts will only be put out for tender where incumbents failed to meet performance criteria. While providing an environment conducive to long-term investment, this will also have the effect of freezing the existing structure of provision. The alternative solution as we see it is not to inhibit new entry or expansion but to provide viable financial incentives to stimulate providers to enter more willingly into the field of adult career guidance.

In this paper we have argued that career guidance services for adults have an important role to play in a labour market which is becoming increasingly turbulent, and in which interrupted spells of employment, unemployment, retraining and reskilling are becoming a more common pattern of career for many individuals. Both vocational and educational guidance need to be given more prominence if they are to support the participation of individuals in a more complex, knowledge-based 'learning society' which such changes involve. Alongside these labour market changes, the organisation and structure of the career guidance system has been changing too, in quite radical ways. As yet, however, these changes have not resulted in a comprehensive expansion of lifelong guidance services which could meet the needs of individuals facing rapid and unexpected changes in their career path through adult life. Current strategy, as for the last decade, remains geared to the skill-growth model of the learning society, in which public provision of guidance services are justified only in relation to narrow economic criteria. Personal career development remains the responsibility of the individual, and social integration considerations are rarely addressed. The provision of adult guidance services remains patchy and inadequately resourced even in terms of the conventional approach. There are severe problems of funding which is increasingly managed through private fees, and problems of access for disadvantaged groups appear to be of little concern to policy makers. In contrast, the core labour market is much better served by a number of large employers who engage outplacement agencies, and by the state in the provision of guidance for graduates from higher education. If an informed choice of the new learning and career opportunities of the future is to become a lifelong concern of the majority of the labour force, much more attention will need to be given to the provision of a comprehensive adult guidance system for the learning society than it receives today.

Acknowledgements

The research on which this paper is based was funded through the ESRC Learning Society Research Programme. We are grateful to Tony Watts and Cathy Bereznicki for their helpful advice at various stages in the project, although responsibility for any errors or omissions rests entirely with the authors.

References

Bartlett, W. (1996) 'Careers guidance and the learning society: quasi-markets for guidance in the UK and France', Paper presented to the 50th Anniversary Conference of the Economics Faculty, University of Ljubljana, 18-19 September.

Bartlett, W. and Rees, T. (1997) 'Financing adult guidance services for the learning society', Paper presented to the ESRC Learning Society Conference, January.

Bartlett, W., Roberts, J. and Le Grand, J. (eds) (1998) *A revolution in social policy: Quasi-markets in the 1990s*, Bristol: The Policy Press.

Burgess, S. and Rees, H. (1997) 'A disaggregate analysis of the evolution of job tenure in Britain 1975-93', Centre for Economic Policy Research Discussion Paper 1711, London: CEPR.

Chatrik, B. (1997) 'Who's running the Careers Service now?', *Working Brief*, February, pp 17-20.

Collin, A. and Watts, A.G. (1996) 'The death and transfiguration of career – and or career guidance?', *British Journal of Guidance and Counselling*, vol 24, no 3, pp 385-98.

DfEE (Department for Education and Employment) (1998) *The Learning Age: A renaissance for a new Britain*, London: DfEE.

Fryer, R.H. (1997) *Learning for the twenty-first century*, First report of the National Advisory Group for Continuing Education and Lifelong Learning, London: DfEE.

Hawthorn, R. (1996a) 'Other sources of guidance on learning and work', in A.G. Watts, B. Law, J. Killeen, J.M. Kidd and R. Hawthorn, *Rethinking careers education and guidance: Theory, policy and practice*, London: Routledge, pp 173-85.

Hawthorn, R. (1996b) 'Careers work in further and adult education', in A.G. Watts, B. Law, J. Killeen, J. Kidd and R. Hawthorn, *Rethinking careers education and Guidance: Theory, policy and practice*, London: Routledge, pp 112-26.

Killeen, J. and Kidd, J.M. (1996) 'The Careers Service', in A.G. Watts, B. Law, J. Killeen, J.M. Kidd and R. Hawthorn, *Rethinking careers education and guidance: Theory, policy and practice*, London: Routledge, pp 155-72.

Le Grand, J. and Bartlett, W. (1993) *Quasi-markets and social policy*, London: Macmillan.

Rees, T. and Bartlett, W. (1999) 'Models of guidance services in the learning society: the case of the Netherlands', in F. Coffield (ed) *Why's the beer always stronger up North? The pleasures and pains of comparative research*, Bristol: The Policy Press.

Rees, T., Bartlett, W. and Watts, A.G. (1999) 'The marketisation of guidance services in Germany, France and Britain', *Journal of Education and Work*, vol 12, no 1, pp 5-20.

Watts, A.G. (1996a) *Careerquake*, London: Demos.

Watts, A.G. (1996b) 'Careers guidance and public policy', in A.G. Watts, B. Law, J. Killeen, J.M. Kidd and R. Hawthorn, *Rethinking careers education and guidance: Theory, policy and practice*, London: Routledge, pp 380-91.

Watts, A.G. (1997) *Strategic directions for careers services in Higher Education*, NICEC Project Report, Cambridge: CRAC.

Watts, A.G. (1998) 'Applying market principles to the delivery of careers guidance services: a critical view', in W. Bartlett, J. Roberts and J. Le Grand (eds) (1998) *A revolution in social policy: Quasi-markets in the 1990s*, Bristol: The Policy Press.

Other related titles from The Policy Press

ESRC Learning Society Series
Series Editor: Professor Frank Coffield

This is a major new series of publications arising from the Economic and Social Research Council's programme of research into *The Learning Society*. It makes an important contribution to the public debate on lifelong learning and will be essential reading for politicians, policy makers, practitioners, academics and researchers. It will help to harness the best ideas in the social sciences to enable the consideration of different visions of a learning society.

Learning at work (1998) Edited by Frank Coffield

This edited collection is important in helping to transform fashionable phrases such as 'the learning organisation' or 'lifelong learning' into practical ideas and methods which could enhance the quality of learning in British firms. The first report in this series examines the key processes of learning, as embedded in particular workplaces, in organisational structures and in specific social practices.
ISBN 1 86134 123 7 £13.99

Why's the beer always stronger up North? Studies of lifelong learning in Europe (1999)
Edited by Frank Coffield

This second report in the series offers a fresh approach on lifelong learning and attacks the consensual rhetoric which has become dominant in the English-speaking world over the last 20 years. It presents models of *The Learning Society*, of lifelong learning and of the learning organisation through cross-national and 'home international' comparisons. It then explores the limitations and advantages of comparative research and will be of particular use to researchers planning international, and especially, intra-European studies.
ISBN 1 86134 131 8 £13.99

Informal learning (1999: forthcoming) Edited by Frank Coffield

The importance of informal learning in the formation of knowledge and skills has been underestimated. Policies to widen and deepen participation in learning need to concern themselves not only with increasing access and appreciating the different contexts in which learning takes place, but also with the different forms of learning. Formal learning in institutions is only the tip of the iceberg and this report constitutes an exploratory study of the submerged mass of learning which takes place informally and implicitly.
ISBN 1 86134 152 0 £13.99

Researching education: Themes in teaching-and-learning (1999: forthcoming) Harold Silver

This highly topical report looks across the traditional education system and wherever else teaching and learning takes place. It looks at schools, colleges and universities on the one hand, and industrial training, nurse and student mentoring, professional development and lifelong learning/learning society on the other. ISBN 1 86134 177 6 £15.99tbc

Adult guidance services and The Learning Society: Emerging policies in the European Union (1999: forthcoming) Will Bartlett, Teresa Rees and A.G. Watts

Adult guidance services, the 'brokers' between individuals and the labour and learning markets, take on a new significance in the context of *The Learning Society* and the end of the 'job for life'. This unique book analyses contrasting approaches to the delivery of guidance services in the UK, Germany, Netherlands, Italy and France, focusing on the effects of marketisation and the impact of European Union policies. ISBN 1 86134 153 9 £17.99tbc pbk
ISBN 1 86134 175 X £45.00 hdbk

All these titles are available from
Biblios PDS Ltd
Star Road
Partridge Green
West Sussex RH13 8LD
Tel +44 (0)1403 710851
Fax +44 (0)1403 711143